FORWARD POETRY REGIONALS 2012

ACROSS THE UK

Edited by Helen Davies

First published in Great Britain in 2012 by:
Forward Poetry
Remus House
Coltsfoot Drive
Peterborough
PE2 9BF
Telephone: 01733 890099
Website: www.forwardpoetry.co.uk

Book Design by Ashley Janson
© Copyright Contributors 2012
SB ISBN 978-1-84418-615-0

Printed and bound in the UK by BookPrintingUK
Website: www.bookprintinguk.com

FOREWORD

Here at Forward Poetry our aim has always been to
provide a bridge to publication for unknown poets and
allow their work to reach a wider audience. We believe
that poetry should not be exclusive or elitist but available
to be accessed and appreciated by all.

For our latest anthology we invited poets to write about
a place or area they are passionate about. The result
is a collection of verse from talented writers that, while
varying in style, expresses and communicates thoughts,
feelings and ideas about regions from across the UK
to the reader. We are proud to present this entertaining
anthology which showcases the joy and inspiration we
can all draw from where we live.

Contents

THE POEMS

A MALVERN MORNING

It is well into September
with the trees already turning
on a ghostly mystic morning
with the sun just breaking through.

On a path hugging the hillside
I approach that certain corner
which I know will open out
onto a panoramic jewel.

I pause and yet again
I silently take in the splendour
of a scene I wish that I could
hold forever in my mind.

But memories evaporate
just like the mists of morning
slowly clearing to reveal once more
our green and pleasant land.

Michael Skelding

I REMEMBER

Empty shops, pound shops charity shops galore
I remember when Stoke us,ed to have much more.
Pottery industry, coalmines and steelworks too
Now we are all unemployed with nothing to do.
Derelict buildings and waste land to let or sell
I remember when Stoke was doing really well.

Stoke used to be special and really make you proud
But now it's a dump with nothing, for crying out loud.
I used to be proud to say I was from Stoke
Outsiders would say 'We know', by the way that I spoke.
It used to be such a great place, it used to have it all
But they always say that pride comes before a fall.

But stoke is now a waste land with nothing at all to give
If I had the chance I would move and find a better place to live.

Lady Sandie Smith

1

BIRMINGHAM BUS TRIP

Hi there, come along and travel with me
On a No. 11, double-decker Bus, Birmingham's speciality.
Join the queue, step aboard, climb the stairs for a grandstand view
Discovering places of interest, I will point out to you.

This bus covers the Outer Circle of Birmingham's large city,
Passing beautiful green parks,
tree-lined lakes and flowers so pretty.
From their garages, they daily travel
a circular twenty-five miles all round,
Taking over two hours, collecting passengers,
so Relief shift drivers are found.

Clockwise and anti-Clockwise,
round and round two routes they drive.
Busy folk pile on with shopping,
and wait for their Stop to arrive.
This red and white bus weaves thru traffic,
for elderly passengers lowered platforms kneel,
Have seats spaces for babies' buggies,
for Mums a special appeal!

The lower deck has a moving picture video,
a calming passenger interest,
But not allowed is eating, drinking or smoking
as clean air is the best!
It is one of the longest British Bus Routes,
first established in 1926
School children are all regulars,
and folk from around the world all mix.
Free Bus Passes for pensioners are really a great boon,
For many unemployed
that Special Day cannot come too soon.
Buying advanced Weekly Passes by everyone,
precious time is saved,
When fumbling or asking folk for change,
travel time is delayed.

There are seventy-one points of special interest
and forty-four fare stages too
Passing three hospitals,
many colleges offering various courses to study and do.
Bournville's chiming Camillon
with forty-eight bells opposite the Village Green
And Cadbury's chocolate factory
with Sports Field and half timbered shops are seen.

Erdington has the oldest pub called '
The Lad in the Lane', fifteenth century,
Winson Green Prison hides behind high walls,
1849 still making history!
Nearby Summerfield School, 1878,
Harborne Swimming baths in use 1923
Some people take the round trip just for pleasure,
make friends, find love amazingly.
I hope this trip with me has given you a memory to store
Come again, there's lots more for you to see and explore.

Now I feel I must mention, it's 2012 it's true
The No. 11 Bus image has modernised
and Harborne Baths are brand new!
When visiting Birmingham
my poem will guide you interestingly.
On the round trip, No. 11 Bus,
you will enjoy historically with me!

Stella Bush-Payne

THE CANWELL SHOW

It's Canwell Show, the day of ego –
The grass is cut, the tents are up,
Cooks are putting their jam in rows.
Farmers' wives bring fruited slabs,
Hedgerow wine and little iced buns.

Growers arrive with champion greens,
Huge carrots and scrubbed potatoes;
Flower folk wallow in their blooms.
Huddled sheep bleat in boredom –
And plump prize pigs behave like pigs.

Later, replete from tent-special teas,
Or sodden by cans of strong beer,
People totter around the stalls.
Others cow-stare and pat cows' heads,
Or admire the jumping horses.

A child bawls as his balloon bursts.
Picking their way through mounds of dung,
The people leer contentedly . . .
They have passed another day.

Sylvia Anne Lees

3

SILENT AGENDA

Pollution, politics, poverty, pain
Job cuts, famine is part of their reign.
Doctors that help the sick to stay sick
Medication next generation as they use an invisible whip
Controlling the mind, blurring the vision
So not to see their destructive mission.

Time to change and open your eyes
Read between the lines and see their lives
Universal angels hear my cries
Unite as one for the love to raise.

Countries in debt, banks without regret
Promises broken, false and untrue.
Government proclaim their here for you
Rebuild a country is what they say.
But they're the ones that made it this way!

Controlling vibrations cem-trails in the skies
We know who you are, we see through your lies
Killing the planet with poison and hate
With open eyes my words will relate.

So out of the box a certain person did say
Out of the box is where I will stay
Conscious, Awareness, Perception too
The CAP of life made for me and you.

Dominica Kelly

DORRIDGE PARK

Autumnal Sunday sunshine ferrets out
family groups whose children flower the grass.
In command, Dad raises the ball to rout
desire for post lunch hours he'd meant to pass
siesta viewing. Harbouring no doubt,
the older children know that Father has
inborn skills as player, coach and scout,
though talent now is claimed by all en masse.
Content that he should show them how it's done,
Mum sees worried toddler run between
herself, where she sits soaking in the sun,
and Dad as he instructs his rowdy team.
Family fun for everyone provided,
but for one small child with parents divided.

Dorothy Ward

WARWICK TOWN

Warwick Castle is a popular place
With concerts jousting and other events
Tourists come from around the world
To soak up its history and then home return.

The castle grounds are lovely too
People have picnics and admire the view
On a summer's day with flowers in bloom
What more could you want, but to smell their perfume?

St Nicholas Park with its flower beds
And the River Avon flowing through
Children come and play ball and crazy golf
And play on the amusement site too.

The children love the train on its tracks
They squeal with great delight
Waving to their mum and dads
It's really a lovely sight.

Norma J Bates

BLACK COUNTRY SACRIFICE

The Black Country history
Its greatness make:
Skies fiery-red,
Foundaries smelting iron
Skies soot-black smoke
From chimney stacks.

Words spoken, we call a dialect,
Have historic aspect
Anglo-Saxon
Words used by Shakespeare
And Chaucer
'Stoon' – stone – in the Canterbury Tales.

Black Country words hard to understand
But in times of trouble
Black Country folk will hold your hond –
Yet, some now request
'Hold my hand'.

Few can agree the Black Country edge
Birmingham, Wolverhampton or Kinver Edge?
But in the Industrial Revolution
The Black Country industry built half the world.

Why?
Women's hands hammering from iron, nails and chains.
A pittance paid
To supplement the menfolk's low-pay,
To feed their hungry crying children
10 or more
Living in Back-to-Back houses,
Brewhouse nail shop on cobbled backyard
Or a chain shop down the way.

In 1910, Mary Macarthur MP
Led the famous women chain makers strike
Six long weeks, no pay,
Battle fought for a better day.
Battle won, a fair wage,
Progress toward today's minimum wage.

Dudley's dark canal tunnel
Three miles long
Beneath world-famous geology of Wrens Nest,
Burly leggers aboard their barges
Legging along narrow brick walls –
Black Country folk strong!

In Netherton, Noah Hingley's foundry,
The Titanic anchor was made –
What a part in history played.

In 2012,
Royal Brierley Crystal
No longer, glass-blown, sparkling bright.
Recession has hit
Hope for many has taken flight.

Now, coal has gone, manufacturing fewer.
The Queen's English trips off many children's tongues.
'Ow bist?' is 'How are you?'
Where do Black Country folk belong?
Don't let your unique dialect die!
Speak as one voice.
You're from the Black Country – rejoice!

Jackie Adams

SUTTON PARK

My favourite place is a bench in the park
A place to be still and to hear the skylark
To lay down my worries and soak in the peace
To learn lessons of trust from the ducks and the geese
Tailor-made living for both water and land
Each day's needs supplied by a provident hand
Watching the ripples of water run free
Reminding us all of how life's meant to be
The trees, tall and slender, sing songs to the breeze
Admission is free –needs no money or keys
The warmth of the sun gently kissing my face
Where on earth could I find a more magical place?

V Smith

SEA OF GOLD

Springtime is here
and welcomes a new sun shining day.
Goodbye to winter let the sun shine,
let the sun shine.
Reflect your beams light up the sky.
Light up the sea of gold.
A vision of colourful blooms take hold.
Golden daffodils take captive
 as delicate petals shimmer and glimmer.

A wave of gold drifting in the breeze
like the pirates gold upon the seven seas.
Trailing along winding rambling pathways
and swaying beneath the trees.
Rippling waves flowing
creating an image of golden waters in a haze.
Drawing ones vision nearer to the magnificent maze.

Daffodils beam and smile up to the sky
waiting for the mixture of sunshine.
Along with a shower of white rain
proudly return upon this earthly plane.
Don't break your golden chain.
The garden is your place to return and bloom again.

Suzette Preston

THE VILLAGE SHOP

The history of many village peoples
was bantered over the counter at
'The Village Shop'.
The hopes and dreams and worries, joys, sorrows and fears
All bantered backwards and forwards at
'The Village Shop'.

Nothing remained hidden,
as the tattle of scandal was laid bare at
'The Village Shop'.
The peoples of the village came to tattle
at the corner shop.
The peoples of the village came to buy
from the well stocked shelves at the corner shop.
Its floor space covered by sacks of potatoes and carrots,
onions and cabbages, apples and oranges,
sugar and tea and endless tattle of tongues.

Wide-eyed children with pennies to spend,
eyes transfixed at the jars of sweets,
aniseed balls and liquorice sticks,
Sherbet dips and ice cream cornets to lick.
Oh! What to pick, can't be quick
Children's eyes gaze up and down,
all around the magic of
'The Village Shop'.

Fliss Edwards

PUGIN'S GEM

Pugin's gem is not set in a stately crown
Nor graces the Houses of Westminster
But nestles in the heart of a market town
St Giles' Church in Cheadle, Staffordshire.

Pugin's gem of a church called St Giles'
A saint who showed kindness to a doe?
A welcoming sanctuary of Gothic styles
Where congregation and pilgrims go?

Pugin's gem built of local blood-red stone
Towering steeple and arms outstretched
Reminding us of Christ's bloody crucifixion
We the people gather to pray out loud.

Pugin's gem is more than a church to adore
A place of contemplation, peace and solitude
The entrance of rampant lions gilded doors
Greets you and guides you into its fortitude.

Pugin's gem confirms the nation shed its skin
Hear the choir sing in thankful exultation
Of dull, plain and painful Puritism
St Giles' architecture exudes magic within.

Pugin's gem points to the heavens above
Some say admonishing those who sin
A pointer of peace in the sign of a dove
Drawing congregation to worship within.

Pugin's gem of a church stands tall
Its foundation decorated with Minton's tiles
The bells ring out from steeple tall
Embellishing these Gothic styles.

Pugin's gem of a church confirms
He came along Staffordshire's Way
With the local people to reaffirm
The Guild of craftsmen left a great legacy.

Cecilia Hill

A COUNTRY LANE IN SHROPSHIRE

I walk along a winding lane where daisies kiss my feet
Where buttercups and celandines say,
Be careful where you put your feet
Because we will glow like sunshine
when the clouds are in the sky
and brighten up the day for you when darkness is night.
Linger by the riverside and hear the water talk
It might just be, 'Hello', 'Goodbye'
I pass this way but once, my journey is never-ending
but I will always quench your thirst.'

Sit down on the green, green grass
and draw your energy from the trees
and watch the leaves all dancing in a soft gentle breeze.

Listen to the orchestra as the birds sing in the air.
Look all around you, take in what is there.

For what you have heard or seen today is never to repeat
But now I am very tired, I think I'll have a sleep.

Shirley Jacks

POTTERIES IN PANCHROMATIC

Jet, silver, rust-iron smiles.
Steel plate images of old life
caught as gift
to future reflections of Hanley's miles
of monuments to survival strife.
Bottle ovens:
crumbling mouths fastening on to charcoal skies;
drawing last-breath gases
from dying industry
and political lies.
But at least we have
exotic ties
to our colonialist guise,
in the vibrancy of the old marketplace.
A welcoming people are we;
who are nevertheless
denied a history.

Linda Rose Turner

RUGBY AND ITS LANDSCAPES

The land around soon comes alive,
Breathtakingly in morning light,
With fields laid out attractively,
Where tree-lined lanes flaunt foliage,
And drifts of shadows overwhelm
One's senses at such images;
Exaggerating country calm –
The Midlands centrepiece on show.

The town's most famous public school,
This beehive of great intellect,
Held rough and tumble games outside;
Which used an oval leather ball
To start a worldwide cultured sport;
And rugger was its common name.

The railway station has this long,
Straight platform that extends so far,
With strange persistence into space;
And echoes with oncoming trains
That thunder on their metal rails.

The River Avon winds its way,
Where past and present overlap;
The onward flow defines itself,
Keeps Nature's themes in harmony.

Upon canal banks anglers sit
Unmoving, poised, with rods held tight;
Eyes focused on those vital floats,
Such charm, such bliss, such faultless peace.

The many villages that stand
So proud about the countryside,
Are islands in these seas of green.

Raymond W. Seaton

SHREWSBURY IN SHROPSHIRE

Walk through this town and you will see
History ev'rywhere
Enabling us to view the past
And 'Then' with 'Now' compare.

There are many Tudor buildings
And narrow passageways
The castle on the higher ground
All link with bygone days.

A flax mill with an iron frame
Was built outside the town –
The finest iron frame in the world
Has gained it much renown.

The Shrewsbury Flower Show attracts
Crowds on each of two days.
There's floral art and famous bands,
Then great firework displays.

Rich countryside surrounds the town
Fields, woods and hills are near.
In ev'ry season as they change
Our hearts are fill'd with cheer.

Summer clothes trees with varied greens
Autumn brings red, brown, gold
Winter's white robe rests on those hills
Spring's new life will unfold.

Walk through this town and you will find
History ev'rywhere.
Then go beyond to nature's realm
Each season's joy to share.

Mary Lacey

COALPORT, OCTOBER

A late last chance for sun brings cyclists out,
bikes skewed on verges, headgear like aliens;
young men sprawl under cornflower sky,
letting the day entice their skins,
pondering – what next and where?

No traffic here, only expended greens
getting the feel for brown. Warm air insists
we could go naked – if we dared
but water's tuning, urgent with gravity,
eager to reclaim ground.

We take the field path, apple-strewn,
needing the river, time's lost idylls
but get algal walls, cars dumped in shadow,
their wintered hulks softened to loveliness, almost.
Below sump-weed runs Severn, muscular,
an olive serpent rolling out from Wales;

no dart of fire, no kingfisher,
but balsam's towering, banked, sweet snatch of spice;
seed flicks my palm when stroked,
fleetingly sexual.

Only a week until the clocks go back.

Marilyn Gunn

FROM AVON TO HOME

From the riverbanks of the Avon they cast their line
Sat in the sunshine, peaceful thoughts come to mind
Ripples in the water, a gentle breeze
Light passing through majestic trees
Dogs in the distance bark their sound
And kids dance and laugh on the merry-go-round
This is so tranquil, I feel at one
But soon to be over for my day will be done
Back to the chaos, the noise well-known
I return to my family, the place I call home.

Steve Allen

THE LICKEY HILLS

With leaves underfoot
And a nip in the air,
Squirrels scampering around
Without a care.
Gathering nuts
Ready to store
Around and around
Gathering more and more.
Days getting shorter
Leaves changing their hue
Winter's approaching
And changing the view.

Anne Williams

THE RED KITE

A red kite wheels aloft the sparkling Saône,
scanning the forest verge. His prey, revealed
only by furtive scurry, forage field
or riverbank where flood, fresh seed has sown.
We, privileged to float upon its foam,
ephemeral as the raptor's pinioned prey,
shall scatter as the seeds the wind has blown
and leave no wake except our DNA.
For sentient life may yet be swept away,
eclipsed by nuclides dispersed by man!
Then Earth shall spin, unheeded, day on day,
and rivers wind where water ever ran.
But sterile – as new lifeforms seek redress
from homo sapiens' appalling mess.

John Burman

OASIS

Along the line of shops,
I weave my way.
Smiling at friendly faces,
Stopping at times to chat;
Exchanging joys and cares,
Sharing our burdens.

Shopping done, across the road.
The green of grass and trees compel
My feet to walk around the pool.
Here ducks and geese and swans are seen.
Pigeons too, reluctant sharers of the crumbs
Scattered by passers-by.

Patient fishermen sit at the water's edge,
Waiting for their first reward.
Memories of long ago rekindle as I watch
Children play on grass, flecked with gold and silver.

Tall poplars pointing up to Heaven
Horse chestnuts, ash and silver birch
Stand in their splendour.

These leaves, these flowers
Breathe Deity supreme.
The willow's whisper is the still small voice of God
Their curtains bending low
Declare how He has stooped to reach us all.
We are without excuse if we recoil
While nature sings its praises
To the God of love.

Rosemary Lander

Gem Of The Albion Town

Sing a song to the Sandwell valley
The gem of the industrial town
of the Albion West Bromwich.
Its rare beauty's a great surprise
To many who don't know it's there.
Many sing of the Albion's fame
In this country which once was called Albion.
Near there where we had an allotment
I felt my heart was there
in the Dartmouth Park and Sandwell Valley.
Don't think that this is all this town has,
it has far, far more to offer.
It has fine libraries, educational need and fine music too,
A Tudor building, the Oak House.
Canals with fishing and boating,
Art galleries, theatres, a zoo on its borders.
There is no excuse for boredom – transport too is good.
This Albion town and its folk are friendly,
their museum shows life as it once was in olden times.
Last of all its pubs are plentiful – and churches too.
So you can take your pick of which most appeals to you,
or even go to both, it's up to you!

Patricia Florence Arnett

Summertime

Well rattle my snakes and go
My cats sing a song for summertime
Women wearing traditional hats
Cuckoo's calling raindrops falling
Children at the mother's side bawling
The sun is shining, the sky's ice-blue
Let's lie in the meadow and feel our love flow through.

Kevin Davies

THE SOUNDS OF MY VILLAGE

The sounds of my village have faded away,
But I can hear them still,
Skylarks rising in Bourke field,
Trill, trilling with a will.

Miner's boots on gravelled road,
Trucks hauling, pit engine puffing,
Rising steam in the sunlight's gleam,
Hail to a beautiful morning.

'Boudicca' gallops in with the milk float,
Tossing her black curly hair,
Proud pony lifting its knees,
Clip-clopping along to each fare.

Ringing sounds from the anvil,
As the blacksmith shapes a horseshoe,
Ding, ding-ding, ding goes the hammer,
Then *zzz* as the quench makes it true.

Time for the school train's approaching,
Hear the whistle, it's almost on time,
Clack-clack, clack-clack, shouts of Gresleee,
Doors slamming, *chuff-chuffing*, sublime.

Monday morn brings the squeal of a pig,
It's hungry cos it hasn't been fed,
Time to change pig into pork,
To the slaughter-house briskly it's led.

The shouts of the tradesmen selling their wares,
On carts pulled by a horse,
What's that pile left on the road?
It's put on the gardens of course.

Mine machinery rumbling below,
They're only sixty feet under.
We hope it will all be worth it,
Will the village be torn asunder?

Banging of bins, stamp of the Shire horse,
Pulling its dust-laden cart,
It's emptying day for the dustbins,
Keep your washing and dustbins apart!

The cobbler bangs away on his last,
Picking the tacks from his lips,
Bang, bang-bang goes his hammer,
As leather to shoe he clips.

It's playtime at the infants,
We hear them shouting, 'Hooray',
The bell ringing clear to start lessons,
Chalk scratches on board day on day.

Hear the loud raucous shouts from the pub
Fill the air on Saturday nights.
Miners have had a good session,
Net curtains part to watch fights.

Yellow cart of the hokey man,
Slowly moving along,
Yellow hokey made into a cornet,
With Rondy singing his song.

The children's choir in the Chapel,
'On a green hill far away,'
The organ notes soaring then fading,
Slowly fading, fading away.

Owen Davies

HIKING

All of the family, we go hiking together,
Walking here, walking there, in all kinds of weather.
With hiking boots and our rucksacks on
Oh, we do have such terrific fun.
We go to Butterton, Hartington and Millers Dale,
And we have walked all the length of the Tissington Trail.
The Peak District is the place to be
For the lovely people and the tranquillity.
The scenery is so beautiful for miles and miles
As we go up hill, down dale and climb over stiles.
From a hilltop we study the view all around
Everything is silent – there isn't a sound.
Only for the twittering of blackbirds, starlings and rooks,
And the trickling of water down by the babbling brook.
As we sit atop a hill, eating our tea,
Each one of us says, 'Yes, the countryside is definitely for me.'

Ruth Warrington

THE RHYTHM OF LIFE

Through the rhythm of life
runs a golden thread of energy beyond compare,
it is found in the world of nature
we breathe it in the air.
To find this precious gift from God,
you need a quiet mind,
to open up your heart
and search for blessings – you will find.
For all around you every day,
in thought and word and deed,
this golden thread of energy
can fill your every need.

You will find it in a sunrise,
the breath of a new dawn,
the quiet certainty that life
renews with each new morn.
Be sensitive to others,
the energy is there,
when you with kindness in your heart
another's care can share.
Explore your favourite flower,
its petals, shape and size,
the beauty and the colour
will increase before your eyes.

Trees also hold this special gift,
seek out their strength and power,
wander in the leafy shade,
enjoy a quiet hour.
Giant oaks, their branches moving
gently in the breeze,
breathe deeply of the clean fresh air
and feel your body ease.
Sunshine lighting, warm and healing –
touch the soft brown earth.
Peat sweat and clean
slips through your fingers,
a gift from Mother Earth.

God filled the world with energy,
to help us every day,
but in the rush and haste of life,
we throw this gift away.
So find a time to be at peace,
away for stress and strife,
and tune into this energy –
'The Golden Thread of Life.'

Cynthia Shum

THE INNER SANCTUARY

Oh to behold the glorious willow
Majestically maintaining its stance
Against the rigours of the elements,
Weeping verdant ribboned foliage
Reaching to connect with the ground beneath,
Cascading leaves a curtain
Behind which is hidden an enchanted excitement,
A secret world of shadow,
Tinted with fragments of sunshine
Patterning this secret cocoon.
An image of two existences
The outer, the inner –
Busy bustling activity, peaceful serenity!
Can this be compared to our lives hidden in God
The outer weighed down with burdens uncontrollable
The inner – an oasis of joy beyond compare
A place of quiet rest!

Doris Bailey

WHERE I LIVE

My address says I live in a city
But I live on the edge of the town
It takes exactly one minute for me to be
In the countryside, where I smile, not frown.

Local villages are close at hand
Where I love to drive and to shop
Handy for charming old inns to eat out
Lovely trees and fields spread out for each crop.

This is the West Midlands, Warwickshire border
In the heart of our soft, rolling greenways
Here it is still possible to stand and be quiet
Where just listening to birdsong is in order.

It's a nice place to live; we've a great service for rail
Also motorways run close, but you would never guess
In this valuable retreat far from hustle and bustle
Of everyday life, always gives me a boost, without fail.

We have beautiful houses and gardens to see
Protected species of wildlife and flowers too
I am really fortunate to live so close at hand
You are welcome to the end of my road, with me.

Sheila Bates

A HAVEN OF PEACE

I love to walk in the peace of the majestic trees
By the tranquil pool, where the fishermen sit at ease.
Not a ripple stirs the surface as the swans go gliding by
And I gaze at the birds flying in the sky.
As I walk along with my dog by my side
Looking at the yellow iris where the ducks try to hide.
We shall walk till we come to a bench in the shade
And we will sit for a while in the peace of this glade.
I love every blade of grass and every leaf upon the trees
And I listen to the sound of the humming of the bees.
Such peace enfolds me as the sun starts to set
As I and my dog and the birds go to our rest.

Joan Painting

THE CROOME CAT

Chevalier is my name
Of very aristocratic fame
With a long history of descendants
Beyond my historic name

Clothes of exquisite smoked velvet grey
Collar designed by Adam
Face of mischievous elegance
And feline grace

Croome court is where I live
Where rat dining is fine
Occasionally a small dormouse
To tempt the palate fine

Crème de la crème, on special days
With beef, pork and fish
Gourmet days always elegant with rich dishes
When one has veal and quail, as one wishes

Satin sheets and velvet cushions
A home for my head
And late at night when really tired
A four-poster bed!

Carol Bradford

THE WILD FLOWERS OF THE LICKEY HILLS

The wild instinctive flowers grow
a perfect expression of God's intention.
Untouched by human interference,
only nature's natural forces mould their shape and habitat.
They are resigned to stay a lifetime in one place
unable to influence outside forces
and as wild, untamed, intricately structured splashes of beauty
are content to add depth to nature's greenery.
These silent witnesses in the midst of active life
unquestioning their existence resemble beautiful jewels
peppering the countryside's unpredictable surface.
Giving food and shelter
to countless living creatures is their purpose.
We are privileged to have such wonders around us.

Audrey Faulkner O'Connor

STAFFORDSHIRE

Staffordshire is a country large and fair
Fields, forests, streams, rivers abound
Hills to the north, weather bold and harsh
Dialect flat, expressive and meaningful
In the south the Trent meanders and widens
Giving pleasure to those by its banks reside.
Crops abound, livestock are fertile
Countryside is lush and soil fertile.
Industry in the north abounds
Population increases because of this.
Roads, motorways, call them what you will
Dissect an area and spoil that which was very still.
Saxons, Norse, Normans were here and held these lands
They left their horde behind.
Paget, Townshenp, Anson, they were all here.
They have stayed and remained for many a year
History is an almanac written about men.
Despatched renewed, again and again.
Staffordshire is still a good place to live
We will always love and care for those who think as we.

Carl Kemper

UTTOXETER MARKET TOWN

Our town is a friendly, lovely place
We have lots of shops for everyone's taste
Doctor Johnson did his penance here
It was pouring with rain and cold I fear
We have lovely cafes to sit and eat
When you have seen the sights with tried feet
Very close, just up the road, is Alton Towers
There are fantastic rides and gardens of flowers
A few miles away are Derby, Burton or Stafford
Bring plenty of money, we have much to afford
The giant JCB factories are all around
Big fishing lakes and ducks can be found
There are miles of walks and things to see
Pastures of green and fresh air is free
Please look on your maps, Uttoxeter is there
We people are friendly, kind and fair.

Glenda Jackson

SHROPSHIRE SEEN

On busy roads there is no peace:
The traffic roars and rushes by.
From north to south, from west to east
The tarmac's groaning in reply.

To running stream and lonely hill,
And ancient introd roots of trees,
There come the Shropshire people still
To seek the peace which each one needs.

Quiescently the cows and sheep
Browse gently in the quiet fields.
The herds and flocks their counsel keep
And do not their own secrets yield.

The badger cubs are winter born;
So soft of fur and short of nose
They venture out one sunny morn
Where no one sees and no one goes.

The Wrekin, at its own behest,
Frowns high above the 'ants' below.
En route for destinations west
Of Wenlock and the Mynd they go.

But those who stay awhile will see
The beauty and the wonders rare.
They'll rest beneath some ancient tree
These quiet Shropshire ways to share.

Dorothy Headland

GRANDAD'S DAD
(The Potteries, Stoke-on-Trent 1950)

When Grandad's dad was a lad
The story of his life is very sad
No computer, TV or lotteries
What a life in the Potteries.

His life was bleak with great despair
Smoke, dust, contaminated air
Kilns, chimneys belching night and day
All his future cast in clay.

Factories or mines his only livelihood
His sole rewards were coughing blood
Coughs, wheezes, colds, sneezes
Not to mention industrial diseases.

He loved his children and his wife
Fought in the war for a better life
He wanted them to have the best
Ignoring the pain deep in his chest.

A pint, a fag, his only pleasure
Clothes off the peg, not made to measure
His life was really very bad
I'm glad I'm not my grandad's dad!

Edward Ashmore

LICHFIELD, CENTRAL REGION

What a glorious sight, as one approaches Lichfield
Ladies in the Vale, three spires, Lichfield cathedral
She has stood there for centuries
On a sunny morning, it lifts your heart
As they shine, like beautiful beacons
To make one feel glad to be alive
Lichfield Cathedral still survives
Bombardment, cannons, fire and the like
She stands supreme, over all she surveys
To brighten up, one's darkest days
For miles away, her beauty shines
From the bottom of our garden five miles away
She's like a lantern, to point our way
Doctor Johnson must have thought this!
As he spent all those hours writing his dictionary
12th century Tudor café, black and white
There coffee and comfort, will put your right
Two lovely pools, Stowe, wide and deep, fishermen and their keeps
Minister pool, swans and ducks, picnic walk, chat and talk
Guild Hall where Lichfield Bower Queen graces all!
Beacon Park, we can't forget, fun for all
Children's play area, games, bring a ball
Pride of place for all to see, Captain of Titanic, E Smith
Surprise one and all, went down with his ship
While band played 'Nearer my God to Thee'
St Bartholomew's farewell, 12th century serene and peaceful
Where one, wants to be, sit and rest, Lichfield at its best!

Irene Grace Corbett

STAFFORD COMMON – SUNDAY MORNING CAR BOOT

(Dedicated to the Sunday morning heroes out in all weathers)

Littered with the detritus of other people's lives
each wonky table a kaleidoscope of memory:
toys a baby threw from its pram
being traded to buy baguettes of ham.
Schoolboys with a come-and-buy look in their eye,
desperate for old Ted to morph into a warrior guy.
Polish, Urdu, French and Shelta voices mingle and fade
into the melting pot of common trade.
A bargain's struck over a handshake
by the proud new owner of a 'vintage' rake
no doubt made in Taiwan last week
with knock-off DVDs' well worth a peek!
Roly-poly mothers haggle over second-hand shoes
crushing bunion toes into phony Jimmy Choos.
Sad stick-thin girls with pushchairs and straggly locks
counting the pennies for ice creams and chocs.
Chipped and sorry, a flying Beswick duck all on its own,
and two rows further on another waits sadly alone,
and right at the end on two twenty-three,
for just 50p, the tiniest duck to reunite all the three.

Stephanie Spiers

HALLOWEEN AT DARLEY

Blind bats scream in the belfry of an ancient Darley church
Where ghostly swaying branches set the scene for the devil with his witches,
Hobgoblins in knee-breeches,
Yes, 'tis the gristly night of Halloween.

The venerable old yew tree in a Darley grave-clad field
Keeps its secrets of the wickedness there's been
Whilst the dancing hags from hell, their ungodly rhymes do yell
On this sacrilegious night of Halloween.

The mossy paths at midnight near an ancient Darley church
Bear the cloven hoofs of demons most unclean,
They pay homage till the dawn brings in the thankful morn
And dispels the devil's birthday – Halloween.

Gordon Smythe

THE MAN WITH THE BRAVE HEART

There he stood, proud in green,
A brave man preparing to be knighted by the Queen.
His battle was over, his fight had passed
But his severe memories would forever last.
The tragic scars would haunt his mind
Scars from the outdated war of mankind.
The man fought hard and he fought strong
He fought for right but also for wrong.
We will forever be in debt to this man you see
This poor, blind man lost more that this sanity.
The man fought for our region and our nation
To try and keep intact our salvation.
On his life the man looked back
And reminisced fighting for the Union Jack.
The man with a brave heart makes my region alluring
For protecting me from the dangers occurring.

Abigail Webb

SPRING (IN STAFFORDSHIRE)

Silver flowers form upon the windows,
As the spirit of the season awakes.
Seedlings and hedgerows stir from their slumber,
Darkness withdraws and light embraces the shadows.
The orange candescence redeems its position on the horizon.

Birds can now sing their dawn chorus
Whilst the sky still holds the morning moon,
Dandelion clock time, is now abundant,
Butterflies reflecting a quiet serenity.
Colour becomes more endemic, in the garden of Albion.

A soft warm zephyr, takes hold,
And paper kites, float in a cloudless sky.
Lambs in the fields, tails flicking,
Springtime's riposte now beckons.
And on the path of the morrow, stands the dawn, of the year to be.

Roger Barnett

WOLVERHAMPTON

I really do miss Hampton
As it was some years ago
I get lost when I go there
But it's not so often now

Could find my way though then
With my eyes shut anywhere
Madame Clarkes in King Street
Old Market, St Peter's Square

Bodega in King's St
Blue Ball in Piper's Row
I danced at The Palais in Temple St
And the Civis still there I know

The Old Arcade in Dudley St
Snelling's fish shop on Snow Hill
I remember Macfisheries, Dudley St
And I guess I always will

Rosenshines in the Old Arcade
And the Army and Navy Store
Millets too in the Arcade
All sadly there no more

Cosy Lyons Corner house
Tucked in a corner of Queen's Square
It's really great to see tho'
The Man On The Oss is still there

We made our dates in those days
Queen's Picture House steps we'd meet
And you would get a smashin' pint
In Gifford, Victoria Street

There was The Ode Still in King's Street
Harley's Vaults . . . Queen Square
Mind you (if I'm not mistaken)
The Ode Still is still there.

We could stay out dancing
Till all hours of the night
Walk from Hampton to get home
And not a soul in sight

These days you don't feel so secure
Night-time and even day
I'd turn the clock back if I could
Have Hampton back the old way.

Jean Mason

PEACE

Heavy curtains splashed with peony blossoms
frame the scene.
Through the glass the stage is set.
Willow trees trail delicate fingers
across the lake.
A squirrel skips with silent feet
to pass my view
pausing briefly to scratch the soil
for a nut he may have left
in early spring.
A family of moorhens
busily pick about with
pointed beaks
moving with hurried steps
to stop then on my patio
and peer into my room.
The sun has travelled fitfully
across the sky
leaving a golden path
to touch the lake
until the night falls
and lamps are lit
to shine on through the darkness
in our village.

Shirley Roberts

BIDDULPH

(This is a true story)

From Stockport to Biddulph
was a wonderful move.
As we walked up the drive that day
it brought a feeling of happiness,
a feeling of welcome to stay.
The bus drivers here are so friendly,
they greeted us with a smile,
as we held hands on the journey,
it always made it worthwhile.

There are so many places to reveal
so many places to see
on a holiday with the grandkids
was just like Heaven to me.
Fish and chips with lots of ice cream
they liked to go out on their roller skates.
A circus or film that they hadn't seen
or go for a ride on a donkey
for everything was so serene.

Now Eileen has gone, the kids have grown up
now we are so far apart.
I long for her to come back again
for I keep breaking my heart.
Would I do it all again?
I wouldn't change a thing!
For Eileen gave me more than love,
she gave me everything.

Although I know she's gone from me
she will always be by my side.
I would never be without her
for she is my love, my life, my guide.

Ian Proctor

BALLINABEARNA BED AND DAWN

Oh I remember well those nights of soft dark damson hue
The crescent silver moon so close in velvet sky deep blue.
I still can see it clear, it seems 'twas only yesterday
The feather bed on which we slept, up Ballinabearna way.

The dancing candlelight was soft on walls of yellow flowers,
How warm and safe and loved we felt, right through the dark
                                        night hours.
Black ironwork at head and foot, four big bright brassy balls,
'Twas mother's place between us two lie hearing vixen calls.

When Aunty Daisy came to stay, she climbed in at the foot,
Her pink toes then would join us three, our eyes with
                                    sleep half-shut.
When morning came through window small, the rising sun
                                    shone bright,
I'd kneel upon the floor to watch the farmyard getting bright.

Then just with only nightdress on, I'd run to fetch the cows,
Along the white and dusty road, 'neath overhanging boughs.
Past butter-yellow primrose flowers, in green long luscious grass,
Upon each blade hung heavy dew, which shone like polished glass.

Though many, many years have passed
Since childhood country days
Sweet memories stay in my heart
Of Ballineabearna ways.

Mary Lefebvre

STOKE (THE POTTERIES)

Stoke to many a long time music hall joke
A living Hell on Earth about which some witless comedian for fun does poke.
A landscape of steelworks, pits and pottery kilns,
belching out clouds of soot-black smoke.
Alive with 'Lowry' matchstick people, the hardy Potteries folk.
Where the wife was 'Me old duck' and her hubby, just 'her bloke'!
With a unique dialect which we spoke, we didn't talk but 'toke'
'Of that fine fat pig o'er thee'er, it'll mack a fine bit of poke.'

Once this was a land of upland farms and moors
Life was hard, the land poor, it was better to stay indoors.
During the winter months, to dig the marl and surface coal
To burn that coal and cast that clay, to make a pot or bowl.
Then to take the pots to market, to sell to some poor local soul
Until farming became a secondary occupation
Pottery making now, their preferred goal.
Coal was mined and steel made and so the potteries grew
But on the local people, these industries took their toll.
The green and purple hills became blackened soil
Whilst Stoke Valley became a disease-filled, smoke-filled hole.

Changes came, hills and valleys green again,
the land once more awoke
The smoke blew away, skies blue not grey.
Now in sunshine and clean rain the ravaged Earth did soak
The mines declines, as North Sea oil and gas, we did find,
To fire those pottery kilns
And Shelton bar no more, lost through international, industrial war
Cheaper to buy iron and steel from foreign mills
Potbanks, modernised and grew,
less dependent on their labour force
Or set up factories aboard, to use a cheaper labour source.

Now these six towns grow green and prey
So isn't a pity, there's still hardship in our city.
We really need to face the fact
That these old industries won't come back.

It's new ones we need to attract
To tell them, 'Look, our folk are hard-working and real gritty
Come! Let's throw poverty out of our city.'
For with new jobs, they can work and pay their bills
Surrounded by now our green and pleasant hills.
Smoke free, but life's less than a joke
To our unemployed potteries folk here in a restored Stoke!

John Pegg

MY HAPPY HOME

When I wake in the morning
No matter if the skies be bright or grey
I know the birds will be singing in the trees
They will chase any hint of the blues away.

Suddenly I think of my dear friend and neighbour
I know soon she will be coming to my door
She will ask after my health I know she means it too
She'll do all she can to make sure I feel cared for and more.

Then as I look through my window
I see the green green grass
That God gave us, making a wonderful display
There are silver daisies and golden buttercups
This is all the gold and silver I need
To make me content all my days.

What a wonderful place I live in
I am a very lucky person I know
I have love and the beauty of God's world
A life I wish everyone could know.

Irene Barton

ON MORDIFORD BRIDGE

(Whilst living in Hereford from 1904-1911, Elgar was in the habit of cycling to Mordiford, where, leaning on the river bridge, he would watch sheep, skylarks, fish and swans.)

By Severn and Wye, by Lugg and Frome
Sir Edward E was wont to roam.
He'd stop beside a bridge to gaze
deep in the water –lazy daze.

And music came from every side,
from hills and valleys far and wide,
demanding to be written down,
until his head was going round.

So many tunes he was aware
he heard –yet sung by mystic choir
away beyond he fields and streams,
who told of seeing in their dreams
a glorious future for mankind
for those who peace in music find.

Thus Elgar wrote upon his score
while music such as ne'er before
came unto him. A Holy Grail
grew out of river, air and vale.

He sang, he whistled, he wrote, he danced.
A flock of sheep was quite entranced
at such a sight. Their eyes grew large;
for once before they'd been in charge
of those who came to see and hear
a miracle.

But is this fair
that woollies with such tiny brains
should hear the Master's noble strains
before I do?

Yet, as I speak
I hear you say, 'Blest are the meek'
More meek then sheep are hard to find.
Let's go with them where rivers wind
at Mordiford. Maybe we'll hear
Sir Edward's music in the air.

Barbara Young

IN THE SMALL HOURS (FROM MY WINDOW)
(Dedicated to my dear Friend Dot with love)

In the small hours of the morning
That still time, before the dawning
Of another hot and sultry summer's day
If you think that all are sleeping
You'd be wrong and if you're peeping
Through the window, you would see, passing by,
The old dog fox on the prowl
While silent, swoops the swift brown owl
And a weary cabbie stalls, right on the junction
Assorted cats are on the march
Disputing boundaries and they arch
Their backs, a-yowling and a-howling
A thrown boot – a good dispersing function!

Then, all is quiet, and I can pray . . .
'Dear Lord, be with me through the day
Give me the strength to carry on
To be a friend to everyone,
As all my life, You've been my friend
And will be, until my life shall end.
Amen.'

Lucy Williams

MAIDWELL

We gladly live in Maidwell
Where everything is just swell.
It is all about the people
Although we do have a steeple.
We share our vicar Mary as many others do
And we are contemplating a long awaited loo!
Our landlord, Rob, organised a diamond Jubilee celebration
With others helping making it a great occasion.
We have a Christmas celebration in our village hall
Not forgetting our two excellent schools.
Too many things to mention here
Whether cricket or Diamond Jubilee tea to share.
Mark my word Maidwell is the place for us
We even have an hourly bus!

Cynthia Fay

It Snowed In Stoke That Christmas

It snowed in Stoke that Christmas,
Soft white feathers falling to the grimy ground.
The pots and pits were hushed that Christmas,
Work ceased for but a short time.
No steam whistle blasted, a call to work from the potbank,
Nor was heard the distant rumble of passing coal trucks.
Nothing to disturb the joyous mood
For a deep silence lay all around.
In the ancient, dingy churchyard
The leaning, soot peeling tombstones
Such a stark study in black and white.
Somehow echoing the mined black-gold
The heaps of chalk-white china clay
A contrast betwixt a potter's dusty day
And the coal miner's tunnel-black night.
The purity, freshness and stillness,
Subtly, sublimely, suspending time.
The black grime and glowing snow
Made the bleak buildings and blasted landscape
Become a monochrome photograph taken long ago.
A point at which, to an earlier era, one might escape.
Ebony-black bottle kilns, set against the snowy hills.
Appeared like gigantic milk bottles filled with stout.
Their tops, snow-frothed on the point of flowing out.
The pit's headgear appeared like fossil dinosaur bones.
Monstrous remains of some great beast,
Snow, now turned pink by the rising sun
Clung to the structure like butchered flesh.
I feast once more on the scene with youthful zest
That day, Stoke, starkly beautiful at its frigid best.

Julia Pegg

IN WOODLANDS' YONDER THERE

The ash, the beech, the oak, the pine,
The capricious wisps of air.
The enchanting stream that weaves and winds,
In woodlands yonder there.

The willow, the larch, the spruce, the birch,
The misty morning scenes.
The birds, melodic midst foliage perched
In shade of nature's greens.

The blueberries, the elders, the brambles, the dock
The seasonal riches to share
The foxes, the badgers, the ladysmock,
In woodlands' yonder there.

The lilypad frogs on the croaking pond
Soft rains and sun-kissed days
The lofty ferns with outstretched fronds
Down secret winding ways.

The rabbits, the squirrels, the bluebells, the buttercups,
A tranquillity for dreamers to share
A place of serenity for the good in us
In woodlands' yonder there.

Peter Terence Ridgway

THE LANE TO THORNTON

When despairing or sad, my restless feet must go
Down the leafy lane, by babbling brook,
To that lovely lake, with its birds and sandy shore
And that great old church, it's always worth a look.

When happy or glad, my contented heart must go
Down to the farm, by apple tree, and then
To meet with loving folk, to drink and dine
In that old inn, where we'll always go again.

When laid to final rest, my tired body must go
Down to the churchyard, with its perfect view
Of land and lake, amongst the fragrant flowers,
To wait for caring souls to smile at whom they knew.

Janet M Peberdy

NATURE'S CALENDAR

Life asleep beneath the Earth
Darkened by a winter sky
In patient pause for renewed life
   Abiding spring to glorify
     Awake!
New seasons are beginning
There'll be many a new display
Trees now unfold their newest coats
   In the cloak of nature's way

Hosts of daffodils sway proudly
Their charm with beauty bring
This display of noble sublimity
   It's the overture to spring

In the woodland fairs the bluebell
On banks the primrose smiles
And meadows green boast their sheen
   Within the hawthorn woven hedge

Catkin dance to windblown branch
As they catch the morning light
Whilst the glistening bark of the silver birch
   Becomes a backdrop of blazon white

Summer's approach comes, Daisy blooms
Facing high to the sun they seek
When a hand can span a dozen heads
   The season has reached its peak

Sailing clouds on summer days
Fleeting butterflies wend their ways
Bees on errand from their hive
   All nature, vibrant, comes alive

A riot of colour will grace this land
Veiled by a sky of blue
Wealth in splendour be its glorying crown
   This treasure is offered to you
     Soon

Tired leaves spread their carpet around
Scattering wide the multi hue
This is nature's colourful reminder
    The cycle of rest is due

Blushed Holly berries with mistletoe
Will drape in harmony side by side
This is nature's gift – it is her bouquet
    They are the kiss of Christmas-tide.

RL Bennett

WILD WARWICKSHIRE

This county's rolling landscape
On Precambrian rocks to the north
Red sandstone centrally and
Blue lias clay south-east,
Hosts attractive habitats
For insect, bird and beast.

The southern quarry sites of days gone by
Now house the rare small, blue butterfly.
Bird populations in decline elsewhere
Enjoy a welcome claw-hold here.
The lakes and rivers in the north
Are favourites for some types
Providing ideal nesting grounds
For lapwings and the snipes.

So twitchers come observe them
Plus the bittern, barn owl, song thrush and chiffchaff
Amble round our rolling fields and hills
Up through the broadleaved woodlands
In this county of *The Bear and Ragged Staff.*

Dave Brough

NORTH

Alright, I give in. I do live in the *North;*
but only to your self-absorbed uninformed eyes;
for Shropshire is south of Manchester or even Blackpool
so just because you live in the Home Counties
and insist that here we all wear clogs and the women
whitewash their sills on a Saturday (which isn't true,
By the way, you can't get whitewash for Homebase
anymore, you have to use domestic bleach)
and there's another thing, women up here
(Oh, you've got me saying it 'up here') anyway,
they don't wrap their heads in 1940s turbans,
they go to one of the three hairstylists
'A Cut Above the Rest'
'You Too'
'Hair Today, Love Tomorrow'
once a week and shop very carefully for
several days afterward.

Which reminds me, whose home are you proclaiming
as yours? The Queen, Prince Charles, Camilla of Cornwall?
surely Penzance can't be in a home country?
I do admit we're distinctly north of Truro
but that still doesn't make us *North.* We like to think
(And I supposed you do too, sometimes) that we are not just
the Midlands, but we are the English Marches.
not military, or anti-Welsh, but simply on
the western edge of England, and proud of it.
Looking up the map, the rest of England
is North of us.

Geoffrey Speechly

FAREWELL TO A CINEMA

Goodbye old friend,
they have laid you to rest.
No longer the pleasure you gave us
as we enjoyed your darkness.
We, simple we, revelled in fantasy
in good days and in times of stress.
Gone are those days when young,
we met our lovers and friends
which gave us much happiness.
In the gloom we entered another world
of action, fun and tears.
Held hands, smoked our smokes,
which dissolved our fears.
Remember as kids on a Saturday
we sang our club song,
Good citizens when we grow up
and champions of the free!
Thank you Roy Rogers, Randolph Scott,
Buck Jones and Gene Autry,
Thanks again for Movietone News,
Bogart, Cagney and serials that kept us in our seat.
We are older now but still enjoyed
the Newcomers, Gibson, Cruise and Streep.
Soon your old frame will disintegrate
from ball, hammer and bulldozer
But the memory remains and always will
of better days from we the picture goers!

R Cope

ODE TO WARWICKSHIRE

Warwickshire the heart of England;
beats with timeless grace.
Your roads have felt the imprint
of many an ancient race.

The mighty Roman soldiers
have tramped up Temple Hill
a centurion once buried here
guarding travellers still.,

Straight and straight and straight on
is the Roman Way
linking place to place
and still in use this day.

But my favourite pastime is
to take the winding way
cut by early Saxons
bringing home the hay.

Trees of ancient lineage canopy my head
branches whisper songs of forests long ago;
where Normans shouted 'Ty a hillaut'
as they chased the quarry there.

Hunting deer and wild pig
they made our county home.
Roman, Saxon, Norman their names are with us still
breathing in the cool, sweet air of river, wood and hill.

Small hamlets nestle by the fields
great castles large and proud
rise, dominating their surroundings
and still pulling in the crowd.

Where kings and princesses,
queens and earls once entered through the gate;
where Warwick, 'The King maker'
is said by some, decided England's fate.

England's heart extended its reach around the globe,
when Shakespeare, the county's famous son
took up his ink-filled pen to write;
his youthful memories filled with scenes of
                              beauteous Warwickshire.

Our own eyes still can see
the mossy bank and eglantine,
the Charlecote Park and deer,
the spreading glades and deep cool shades
the Avon running clear.

How lucky I am to stand upon
the self-same sward as those
Whose names have made our county great
and set our aims and goals.

Looking up into the same blue sky
as those who have gone before,
I see a small light plane go by
a youth is learning how to fly.

I stand but a moment in time,
between the past, the now and our tomorrows.

Sheila Brooks

FIRE AND BRIMSTONE

They worked the steel
They worked with zeal
The heat of the furnace
And sweat dripping from the face.

Then the Old Level
Where the workers would revel
The trains going to Baggeridge,
Who would envisage.

Round Oak mighty
Supplying steel to the country (and beyond)
To the Earl of Dudley
Making things a reality.

But to be shut down
Under Maggie Thatcher's frown
No more in England
And the 'Beer Carrier' was legend.

Jonathan Luke Simms

BAGNALL VILLAGE

Bagnall village, stands high upon a hill,
I was born not far from the village.
I bet a good many can remember still
I was a bit of a lad and my name is Bill.

The church steeple, points towards the sky
A lot of my relatives are buried in the churchyard.
Many passed away because they were ill,
Others died as they were getting old.
On a winter's day, it can get rather cold.

In the summer, when the sun does shine
You could call in the Stafford Arms, public house
For a beer, a meal or a glass of wine
And drown your sorrows, before closing time.

I've spent some happy moments, on the village green
As a boy with my friends, many things I've seen.
Although now, I'm getting haggard, old and grey
I can very nearly remember that very first day.

I met a lovely lass, we were both thirteen,
We went out with each other for over a year.
After we'd left school, we went our own separate ways
Then, after fifty-three years we met up again
And we've been together now for nearly three thousand days.

I haven't been to the Stafford Arms for quite some time
But, I've remembered it and other things in this rhyme.
Perhaps my friend and I may visit the pub, one day soon
And we can recall, what happened underneath the moon.

William Jebb

MY KINGSHURST COUNTRYSIDE

Stepping out of my front door I wonder on a while
And there it stands before me; it always makes me smile,
My own piece of countryside, a special place to be
Come, walk along beside me, I'll tell you what I see.
On our right we pass Yorks Wood, dressed in leafy green
Like a gateway to a fairytale in a long forgotten dream,
We stand upon the first small bridge, beside its friend, the tree
Below, a stream flows right to left, to a lake far as the eye can see.
The path leads to the second bridge that stands besides Babbs Mill
Beneath us flows the river Cole, always flowing, never still.

We turn right there are fields and ponds, the path of green goes on
Now we have to make the choice, turn right, turn left or carry on.
On is the path to Gressel Lane, arched with trees on either side
Left, we have another choice, around the lake or riverside.
Today we choose the river, so over the bridge and turn
A heron stalks and swans glide by; see how their young ones learn
We pass the copse of trees so tall, our journey carries on
Past lines of oak, old sentinels, that span the years of life
                                            now gone.
They guard the rear of Sheldon Hall, all steeped in history
You still can see the splendour of the way it used to be.
On our left the river runs kingfishers dart, electric blue
Right stands the crow tree stark and bare,
Once burnt but still stands tall and true
Now the lake rejoins the river,
To the playground bridge we journey on
We could cross over, return to home,
Or take the path that carries on.
To Cooks Lane Bridge then Chelmsely Wood
Miles and miles to who knows where
Walking on forever, in this place so fine and fair.
Birds of water, birds of sky,
With eyes closed tight we stand and hear
Midges, bees and butterflies, the world of nature, ever near.
I hope you enjoyed our journey, as we walked side by side
On the paths of my inspiration – my Kingshurst countryside.

Cal Pearson

Evesham – The Swans Upon The River Avon

The swans along the River Avon
So graceful, so at ease
Gliding along the water where they belong
Upon a summer day, not a cloud of grey.
Watch them from the bridge
Watch the day drift by.
The swans so regal, so divine
Their long necks, in a group
Loving the sunshine
Hear them hiss so loudly.
The swan upon the River Avon
Where time stands still
A breeze through the trees so timeless.
We sleep upon the water
Our beak inside white feathers.

Barry Powell

An Old Inn

Down a quiet country lane
I stood beside an inn
Its windows all of mullioned pane
Its curtains thread-bare thin

Blistered doors at crazy angles
Beckoning to the last
Everywhere are cobweb tangles
Hiding a lurid past

And climbing up the ancient stair
Which buckled shoe has trod
I feel mine host is standing there
To give a friendly nod

These walls have many to tell
They've echoed loud and long
To the clash of steel when Roundheads fell
For singing Cromwell's song!

Robert Stevens

THE RIVER SEVERN

People wave from the Ironbridge
A little shop fills full of people buying gifts.
A boat tug, tug, tugs through hanging trees.
A breeze blows and leaves fall like confetti.
A fisherman waits upon a ledge for a catch.
Hikers walk through a herbal path and a scent fills the air.
Children's voices echo across the river as an ice cream van
                                        draws near.
A dog makes a splash jumping in the water.
A willow tree shades along the water's edge.
An otter's face appears then disappears just as fast in ripples of
                                        moving water.
Sun beats down through the trees and I close my eyes like it's all
                                        a dream.

Jean Bailey

LEEK TOWN

Home within the heart of moorland peak
Lies the story and town that's Leek.
So many lives, layered through time
In local history of this market farmer's town, do rhyme.
Its people salt of the Earth
Live lives of legend – quietly, busy, loud, heroic – with mirth.
Streets well-worn by farmers, townsfolk, visitors –
Strangers of distance and of locality.
A rich tapestry of many – a bustling richer reality.
The Nicholson War Monument stands for sons passed into history
Testament of lives of courage and sacrifice –fate's mystery
St Edward's Tower, Trinity, St Luke's and St Mary's
Church spires stand – for all in birth, marriage, death –
Prayer and faith – on this ancient land.
Shops, pubs, cafes up and down
Where characters walk these streets –
Out from the hills, in through Leek's town!
Steeped with history and old ways,
Beneath the monument's clock face move all Leek's days.

Paul Holland

THE DERELICT STATION

Uncared for and dejected, there it lay,
Listening and dreaming, day by dreary day
Sadly pondering the reasons why
Its platforms now lay open to the sky
Muddy pools were to be seen
Where hurrying feet there once had been
Surrounded by the city's constant roar
Remembering the days of yore
When laughing children travelled to the sea
As, of irksome school they all were free
And people saying their goodbyes
Felt cinders flying into their eyes
And nearby, subterranean passages were
Where ghostly voices filled the musty air
Hidden now from incurious sight
They no longer led the way from dark to light
Were lost, beneath department stores
And remained a place for honoured past to pause
And sigh, because man's schemes
Made them forget its heritage of dreams.

Florence Barnard

THE HONEYSUCKLE DELL

It haunts me still. It lives within my mind,
A vision of a honeysuckle dell
Floating on waves of heat that rose and fell,
Where we could love and leave the world behind.
Sweet were the woody climbers as they spread
Their lavish sweep of flowers pink and yellow,
Sating the mothy vines with fragrance mellow,
Aglow with burnished berries fiery red.

I saw it only yesterday but found
To my dismay a dark and dismal scene.
Winter had drained all colour and the ground
Was hard with ice and gone was all the green;
A lonely place with silence all around
And I was lost in thoughts of what had been.

Celia Thomas

WORCESTERSHIRE

Bird songs trilling at the break of dawn,
Church bells ringing on a Sunday morn.
Daisies, buttercups, embellishing the lawn,
How could things get better?
Six generations, for a barbeque gathered,
All safely in our own garden, tethered.
Old ones, young ones, enjoying things together,
How could things get better?
Apple orchards grape and pear
With what else can these compare?
These bounteous things from God's own hand
How could things get better?
The rolling hills, the vista's fair,
From top of hill just stand and stare.
All green and gold, by God's hand watered
How could things get better?
Oh! Worcester, rural jewel in the crown
Fair and beauteous have you grown
Ne'er was a place of such renown
Things just could not get better.

Joan Wheatcroft

TREBANOS

Trebanos, a small village
Deep in the heart of Swansea valleys
There is a peace here
That is so nice
A wood to walk in
A waterfall and canal and river
That flows to the sea.

I love Trebanos
I would not leave
To see such a lovely place
So peaceful and friendly.
So thanks to God for Trebanos
It will stay in my heart and soul.

Robert James Lewis

SCOTLAND

No matter where I wander, no matter where I roam
I'll always think of Scotland, the place I call my home
I love the dear land because it's so fine
I love all the people because they are mine

To be in Glasgow it seems just right
Fills my heart with joy and delight
Around the world there's famous scenes
But none like Scotland land of my dreams

The land of glens, home of the kilts
The land of songs with lovely lilts
The land of poets, land of burns
The land where my heart will always return

The land where the weather's not always nice
Surely if it where it would be paradise
The land where my heart will always lie
The land I'll live in till I die.

Gerald McLean

PEAK DISTRICT

We abseiled your rock face at Windy Edge,
Stoney Middleton, facing our fears and letting go!
We walked in the dampness and darkness of Bagshawe Cavern,
tears and panic we overcame!
We walked your hills and valleys
 and canoed your waters from Darley Dale to Mattock Bath.
Every moment was beautiful,
breath taking and exhilarating!
There is so much of his Peak District left to explore!
The more we delve into your majestic beauty
the more we realise that Heaven is a place on Earth!
So when your rocks crumble and fall,
your rivers rise and rage, caves flood and silt flows,
we honour your raw power and stand in awe!

Rachel Jane Dando

IMPRESSIONS OF THE RUINED ABBEY AT CROWLAND

Once a mighty abbey stood in this place
but now majestic ruins fill the space,
the front has carvings from a bygone age
just like a scene with stone stains on a stage,
no huge oak door or fine windows are there,
the finery's gone, the stone walls are bare.

The nave's ceiling's now an expanse of blue
where clouds like angels pass over anew,
magnificent archway, unbroken span
despite attempts at destruction by man,
a staircase leads nowhere seen up on high,
steps only lead onwards into the sky.

A sound of singing is heard on the breeze
but only the rooks are cawing in trees,
low whispers are heard of monks at prayer
turn around quickly, there's nobody there,
here in this place, the spirit of goodwill,
holy meditations echoing still.

Gillian Jones

OUR SHAMBLES IN YORK

In the quaint city of York
The Shambles has a famous walk
Here among the cobbled street
Are shops in line to greet
Heritage, architecture and mystery
Each one with its own history
A magical street tucked away
But people flock to it every day
All wanting to be a part
Of the Shambles they take to heart.

Dawn Moore

THE PLACE WHERE I LIVE

The place where you live should be full of joy
A place that is contentment for each girl and boy.
Happiness should ooze from every home
And mums and dads there, to stop kids feeling alone.
But life is not like that in this digital age
People are living on a minimum wage.
Jobs have been cut and pleasures are few;
But people where I live know what to do.
Wall Heath is the village where I live,
A place where most are eager to give
Support to the lonely, charities and such
And always time, where it's needed so much.
Plenty of interests and one or two clubs,
Townswomen guild and also some pubs.
Three churches supported by the villagers too
And sporting venues are always in view.
Plenty of walks are used by many
The canal, railway walk and parks – so many
Lots of active things to do.
No time for boredom – enjoy what you do.
The schools in the village have a good name
And youngsters are bussed in – outside our domain.
Education's important – good staff even more.
It's good to know that jobs are secure.
Our village is edged by other villages too
The countryside to Kidderminster is also on view.
Buses to towns are a frequent sight
And the many passengers – a chattering delight.
Well! That's our village and where I live
So much to do, so much to give.
A wave of the hand, a smiling hello
The people of Wall Heath – *a pleasure to know.*

Elizabeth Timmins

MY BELOVED ARTHUR

I had a precious sweetheart
Who was all the world to me
I loved him from the moment
He kissed me tenderly

I remember days of courtship
A gentleman was he
When he kindly introduced me
To his friends and family

We made our vows together
We meant every word we said
'To love and cherish each other'
From the moment we were wed

The years pass all too quickly
Days of happiness and glee
Also grief and sorrow
That comes to every family

Now this beloved sweetheart
Has left this earthly realm
To be with his precious Saviour
Who was his Redeemer, Lord and friend

Sometimes the days are lonely
From his photo, he smiles at me
And when I read his Bible
Truthful words I see

One day the Lord is coming
The dead in Christ will rise
The saints will be reunited
In our Father's paradise

For the trumpet will sound so clearly
And those who love the Lord respond
In the twinkling of an eye
The Lamb has summoned His blood-bought children home.

Doreen Mary Reeves

CITIES

London, Birmingham and Hull
Reading, Oxford and Leeds
Cardiff, Bristol and Swindon
But better than all of these
Is Herefordshire because . . .

The sun shines bright over Herefordshire,
The red warm earth awaits
Bounteous crops of apples and hops
And the brilliant yellow rape.

The Wye meanders through Herefordshire
Tintern, Ross and Hay
And flows by Whitney, Fownhope and Chepstow
As it wends upon its way.

Herefordshire is the place to be in
Set in the marshes of old
The Golden Valley with its beautiful views
Is simply a joy to behold.

Celia Brown

PERSHORE TOWN

I've lived in this market town
for over thirty years or more
with a splendid abbey and Georgia homes
and interests by the score.

We are tucked in the Vale of Evesham
surrounded by field and farm
with a college of horticulture I thank God
I've been blessed with so much charm

We have a farmers market
and we are proud of our Pershore plums
village pubs lie all around
serving their own ale and rum

In the distance lies Bredon Hill
gorgeous woods like in-between
visitors come and go all year
saying, 'What a super town we've seen!'

Alison Jackson

THE MALVERNS

On a bright Summer's day you can see for miles
From climbing up the hills and stiles.
The sky may be azure or grey
But the hills and valleys slope and dip
In perfect English array.
Schools of children gather there
When summer breezes blow and weather is fair
All walking in the contented glow
Of these Beacons, and heather growing everywhere.

Elgar's music was inspired
When he was walking amongst these hills.
Such inspiration fired
By watching, observing and standing still.
These panoramic views
Are to be seen, if you choose,
From the Beacon.
In Summer the butterflies flutter amid the bright gorse flowers
And the adders lie out in the sun-baked sand paths.
Green ferns adorn the earth while up above the kestrel hovers
And larks sing, as if to herald the new found Season.

From the top of the Hills, the surrounding Towns
And buildings look like midgets, they seem so small.
But the view is panoramic and not limited at all.
You can see the three Counties from the Worcestershire Beacon
All the Schools, Colleges and Churches lie in the valley unawoken
It is so exhilarating to be high up there
With the wind in your hair, to leave your cares behind you
And to walk through ferns and gorse and bracken.

Hilarie Grinnell

THE MIDLANDS

In this crowded town, solitude
and quiet beauty can be found
at the bottom of my garden.
This secluded spot, wrought by hands and seasons
was always dear to me and this hedge too,
that stops the Canadian geese and their brood
coming through, yet letting me view the pond
seething with life, where gilded petals
expand, its banks studded with daffodils.
On the island geese hide to hatch their eggs.
A thick wood surrounds the pond and my garden,
shutting off the far horizon. Higher up a playing field
hides the road, muffling any sound.
As I sit and look at the sky,
shared by oak tree branches and a spire,
I scan with my mind's eye unending space,
and depths of quietness echo in my heart.
And, as I hear children's voices and the wind
whisper among these trees, to my mind
there comes eternity, the past seasons
and this that is, alive and now, the sounds of it
echoing in my fluttering heart.

Angela Matheson

DOWNTURN

The old town was dying
Between the slabs
And weed grass gaps
Of shuttered shops,
Once prosperous in our prance –
Until the signs tied the sinking knot,
Broke the stricken noiseless glance –
Now, desolate of face like so many silent cogs
Rootless, floats the open door of hope,
Awaits – perchance – like the airless grass.

David Lloyd-Howells

HIS SONG

It is the magic time
When our robin sings
By the street lamp
And under the moon!
His song of enchantment
Fills the air!
Beautiful warbles
And trilling of notes!
The world is asleep
It does not hear
His song!
But it matters not!
For he sings on
Without a pause
And sings and sings
For evermore!

Veronica Twells

DIPPERS IN THE REDLAKE RIVER

Along the riverbank – fast flowing –
bobs the dipper, seeking fare
for her babies, grey and fluffy,
waiting in their hidden lair.
'Neath the waterfall, full hidden
from all dangers lurking near,
happy in their moss-lined corner,
cosy now and free from fear.
Faithful parents always bobbing,
diving, swimming, in and out,
seeking food 'neath rocks and pebbles,
up and down and round about.
Over rocks and under dark boughs,
bright the merry water swirls,
singing, splashing, gaily laughing,
forming bank side droplet pearls.
But the dipper, madly searching,
has no time to stand and stare –
we, more fortunate, may stay there
watching them without a care.

Iris Greaves

BIRMINGHAM

It's a place I have admired
Always it's been there
Places I see
Places I remember
Faces of people I know
The place I call my own
This is Birmingham,
This is my home.
No matter where I am
Or wherever I go
I will always know
This is the city
That created me.
My language, the way I dress
Even influences the music I listen to.
Because of this place
This is what I've now become.
Birmingham, I call you my own,
This is my place,
This is my home.

Trevor Hussey

DARK CLOUDS

We awoke to a wonderland around the Clees today
A sparkling white carpet softened our way,
A wealth of diamonds winked from the eaves
Jack Frost had been busy, he knew how to tease.

I remember a winter in days of old
When snow was deep and the wind blew cold
Snowdrifts hid the high-hedge top
And war-time prisoners cleared a way to the shop;
A country mile we had to go
Through narrow walkways dug in the snow
Passing places were made here and there
But no one around for our trials to share.

We were fighting a war to end all wars
And before my time we fought the Boers
Now it's Afghanistan in a plight
And again our lads are called to fight
They lose their lives in another's cause
And return in a coffin amidst sad applause.

The clouds above darken and dark clouds cry
When we ask the question, 'Why, oh why?'

Nora M Beddoes

WORCESTER CATHEDRAL

They are light-petals
as if windblown
winding down
lights dancing
on the empty floor
of the cathedral

Light-motes green
green gold amethyst
floating sunlit
photovolts
of silence
on the tidal reach
of geometric marble
emptied except
for the quiet tread
of gaze-about visitors

Dappled in the confetti -
fall of lit moment
illuminating
skirt sleeve skin
that will go with them
from this gleam
of morning unto
the lengthening afternoon
of their pilgrimage

John Alcock

JANUARY WALK

(The River Wye near Brampton Abbots)

Three ash trees growing as one
On a hill of close-cropped grass.
Room here to breathe to feel the air
Sing, the earth answer, warm with
The labour of centuries: hedgerow,
Woodland, field after sloping field

Reclaimed from wilderness
For sheep, cattle, crops. Swans rest
In the turnips along the water's edge.
And at a bend in the river
An iron memorial recalls a man
Who gave his life saving two children

From the current's serpent sweep:
Ceaseless motion embracing joy
And tragedy and as constant
In change as the hurrying clouds
In the wide sky, or the slow-turning
Seasons, or human activity itself

For all its straight lines: the railway
That once spanned the river here now
A vacancy of air, its embankment
Abandoned to brambles, then cleared
For ramblers. A quiet landscape,
Gathered up in its own storied wealth

Of stillness.

David Donaldson

POOLSBROOK COUNTRY PARK

When I was a young lad the coal lakes were black
From the mountains of slag that loomed round our back
The brook ran sluggish, gorged on coal and slack
Now wild geese fly in from their roosting
Over tree-cloaked hills and scrub-scrappy grass
To land on clear shining waters redeemed from the grimy old past

The moorhens are squabbling for a place on the island
As swans float serenely by or flute in on singing wings
Hares are now boxing on secluded pathways
That snake around dark-historied hills
Here, where once pit managers tallied their quotas
And planned our working days
We now count magpies amongst wild flowers
That glory in disordered arrays

Perched in the early mist, on the power-line staffs
Are the crotchety crows and quavery starlings
The short-resting sparrows and plump coda pigeons
They all write the dawning pastoral symphony
Ephemeral phrases, constantly never the same
The swallows are dancing to his restless refrain
And move ever and endlessly over the lakes

There'll be trout soon in the lower stream
Fanning over limestone beds
Where the bulrushes are spreading with their inexorable tread
Their bobbin heads are bending in the same wind
That blew in years before
Over groups of huddled men,
Waiting at the pithead for the morning – draw

There's an old cobbled path back bowed for the storms
That ambled past hay-wains and hedgerows to a hilltop farm
The hay-wains have gone but the farm still remains
With stones that are made concave and wrinkled with age

We walk there now, already foot-notes to the past and
Know that the ages of man were never built to last
The tides of the countryside remain as a variations refrain
To the Babel of progress whose echoes must fade.

Steven Haywood

LEICESTERSHIRE – SOMETHING FOR ALL

Leicester is good for learning,
a university second to none.
Students come from far and wide
surely a benefit to everyone.

Leicester is famous for its Walkers crisps,
with various flavours all to please.
Melton Mowbray pork pies too,
all your appetites there to tease.

There's a folly standing in Leicestershire
known locally as Old John.
Tall and shaped like a beer mug,
it's a sure sight for everyone.

It stands on a hill in Bradgate Park,
a beauty spot used so well.
Surrounded by herds of deer,
history of Lady Jane grey as well.

The Hanson cab was invented
in a Leicestershire market town.
In Hinckley it is all recorded
the history is all written down.

There's a famous theatre in Hinckley
known as Concordia by name.
They come from miles around the country
to see many productions gain fame.

They say it's the centre of England,
for others it's simply not true.
Known as High Cross, found on the A5
it's there for all to view.

Leicestershire's the place to be living
with museums, parks and theatres too.
Try taking a trip by train or car
and enjoy pleasures to see and do.

Margaret Meadows

DISCOVERING MALVERN

My youth was spent in London
To me, nowhere could have been better.
I married a Royal Air Force husband
We got posted – more times than a letter!
Always moving from place to place
There was so much to discover.
Then, in retirement, we had to find
A new home just for each other.
After searching for nearly two years
In Worcestershire we found
Malvern. So peaceful, no aircraft sound!
We saw Malvern Hills and we were sold!
Just knew then we had to live there.
We found a house on that day too
Thirty years on and I still live here!
Never have I wanted to move away
Though now I'm old and alone.
I love the Malvern countryside
It has become my home!
All kinds of birds, squirrels and trees,
Lovely villages, towns and scenery.
Shops for all you could possible need
Plus bluebells amongst all the greenery!
Good roads for traffic
Plus peaceful byways
Friendly people who stop to chat
Patches of woods filled with daffodils
I love to stand and look at that!
Not able to go out, unaccompanied now
People wave to me through the window
One or two join me for coffee or tea
Which always makes my heart glow
For alone, I often get lonely.
The garden is now my source of pleasure
I watch all the wildlife
At times of leisure.

I can't tend the gardening anymore
Though it always pleased me to do it
A gardener now does it for me
It's my joy just to walk through it!
I think of the day we found Malvern
With gratitude and grace
I will live here now to the end of my days
It is really such a delightful place.

Mary Eagle

A RANGE, ARRANGED

'You've seen one hill, you've seen them all,'
There's some who take this view
But, looking at the Malverns,
It simply isn't true.
If I've been touring for the day
However far I roam
Once I see the Malvern Hills
I know I'm almost home.
Or, I can be, upon them,
With miles and miles of view,
Stretching out, before me,
To thrill me, through and through.
Not for me Grand Canyon
Andes, Pyrenees
Malvern has the unique way
To emulate all these
And, even if I journeyed,
To look at all the rest,
They May be nice, but I'd still claim,
The Malverns are the best.

William Umbers

DROITWICH AND THE SURROUNDING AREA

Walking the paths of Droitwich Park,
looking at the scene,
where the rockers and the hippies fought
is now a bowling green.

Redevelopment, the planners say,
as they build their factories where old
droitwichens did play,
Vines Park has taken its toll with the
changing of the time,
with ergonomics changing the environment
will the church bells play a different chime?

Around the park walls to Westwood Lake,
where beauty stares you in the face,
over Jacob's Ladder to Hadley Wood,
pausing at the spring by Hadley Mill,
where wild birds of every kind
give off their friendly shrill.

The farming community of Ombersley
are real good country folk,
tending their fields for harvest time,
their minds are full of hope.

For peace of mind we go to Ladwood,
around Martin Hussingtree,
with its green fields and open spaces
it's serenity.

Standing in the midst of this land of bliss
lie the 49 steps at Salwarp leading to a life
that I once knew,
where one could breathe the fresh air of spring
and listen to the chorus of birds sing,
or sit and watch the fishes glide
in the safety of their River Salwarp hide.

At Hanbury Wharfe not very far,
where everyone can see,
boats are moored for pleasure,
while Brummies fish merrily.

On down the road to Shellford,
where the winding brook winds by,
on through Himleton, a sleepy village nigh,
at Crowle village there is the old Checques Inn,
where one can stop and natter in.

Or walk down to Dunhamstead,
passing woods and orchards on the way,
over the railway crossing to the old canal,
pausing at the country inn,
where they have some tales to tell.

Still we are moving forward past Oddingley
to Shernal Green,
where deep thoughts in my memory
bring back a peaceful dream.

As we travel round through Hadzor
we are nearing Droitwich Spa,
to think I used to walk around these places,
now I travel everywhere by car.

John Hickman

HEREFORDSHIRE AND THE WYE

The Wye, a sporting river in the past
Assumes new life with quite a different sport
Canoes now join the salmon drifting past,
An interest to which all can resort.

Along the banks lie many fertile fields
Where livestock graze – though not so many now
Potatoes, corn and apples – better yields –
Aesthetically inferior to the cow!

Our great cathedral sits upon its banks above
Where nearby, Elgar lived for quite a while
His wondrous works of empire, joy and love
The Enigma – to make us think and cry and smile.

Our glorious countryside has got the lot
Small towns and villages all set in lovely land
Each settlement with the reminder which it got
When brave souls died to see that it stayed grand.

So there it is – our shire and river too
Beloved by we the lucky ones who got here by our birth
Now welcome those that we call 'new'
To join us on our favourite piece of Earth.

J W Mokler

MY BEAUTIFUL CITY

The region I live in is my favourite place
Nottingham, lots of history and a very busy place
Sherwood Forest near at bay
Robin Hood was here as well to stay!
Our castle, a museum are works
Of art and that's just a start
Lace Market in all its glory
Galleries of justice, dungeons to see
Prisoners were kept there, for small crimes
Taking an apple from a cart
Notts Forest, also County
Two football teams, just naming a few!
Brain Clough stands in the square
A sculpture to remember, he was here
Trip to Jerusalem, The Bell
Inns from years past
They really are the best
Nottingham's the best city in my eyes
I love it and very proud.

The River Trent many hours I've spent
Trips on a boat to relax
Seeing monuments from the past!
 Shopping centre with lots of shops
My region is superb
But not another word
I love it so
You'll have to go!

The Major Oak where Robin Hood's men used to stay
Little John and all, his Merry Men had a rest
And off they'd go again.
Torville and Dean were born here, great prestige for our city
Paul Smith his clothes, stand proud in the town
The Bell Inn with its caves stretching underground,
Great history to see

Trip to Jerusalem old worldly pub, 12th century
We had the Queen here just last week,
Thousands turned out to see her wave from the balcony
A beautiful day, she seemed so happy!
 A relaxed field games for old and young,
Will and Kate enjoyed it too.
Nottingham is my favourite place, lots of history and grace
I've visited many cities, beautiful as they are
I love Nottingham the best by far
Memories when small, trips to Theatre Royal to see a show
Nottingham Arena now we've got the Ice Stadium and more
I could go on forever with this story
My heart is here and always will be.

Pamela Hawksley Blackburn

BOSTON STUMP

The church doors, 7 in number
Are somewhat easy to seek,
They represent Sunday and Monday
And the other five days of the week.

The steps which go up to the library,
Make me wonder far more with dismay,
To think there are 24 of them
Corresponding to the hours of the day!

The stairs to the chancel are 60,
Showing Man's architectural skill,
Calculating the minutes and seconds,
Showing the hours for your work to fulfill.

There's something about our grand old Stump
It's an almanac, quite clear –
Her steps numbering 365
Which relate to the days of the year.

Her windows they number 52
Which serve for the weeks in the year,
The pillars number 12, you will find,
Giving us the calendar quite clear.

Esther Hawkins

THE SECRET GARDENS OF HEREFORD CATHEDRAL

(Dedicated to Dr Anthony Evans and his Wife, Elizabeth and all the voluntary helpers in Hereford Cathedral's Gardens, friends of the Cathedral)

The Cloister House Gardens
The cathedral gardens woven emblems of nature's love
Here holy walls accept the crumbling touch of time.
I feel a melody, an understanding music from above.
A gardener stands, a gentleman, English – a face so fine,
His classic straw shades his skin from the summer sun.
A clock chimes and seems to say 'Thy will be done'
He moves and gently leads his band to work and understand.
Grass, flat, epitaphs in stone lie beneath my feet.
In memorial, washed by rain and dried in summer's heat.
Scattered tables rest, people sit and muse,
Social smiles, pensive thoughts, happy families meet.
Around the arbours of remembrance this garden blooms,
Youths unfading roses climb, bursting buds to open soon.
Hostas, lush and green; fragrant lilies, stems growing tall,
Oh warm sweet breath of June, pale greenery unfurls.
Conical cream hydrangeas flushing pink with time,
White daisies and poppies, seeded nasturtiums romp in line.
A moth rests on the grey-green leaves of the catmint,
Aromatic flowering true,
I see the lobed leaves of the geranium, her flowers honest and blue.
On the corner stands the Glastonbury Thorn, wise, old and worn,
How long have you been here? What have you seen?
Your brittle branches, dear old cathedral tree,
Fable or tale? 'Tis no matter, you breathe a faith in me.

Chapter House Gardens
Now in the passage of the vicar's choral, a cool retreat,
Centuries past, years of change; the mystery of time
There is a balance, trusses, old hammer beams,
Shadows of the past flutter and unfold.
A garden, within four walls of stone, beneath the ceiling of the sky,
Plants and shrubs in shade, assuming a church-like air.
A formality, drawing a blind on surrounding space,
In the midst a fountain's falling water flows with grace,
Mosses and ferns cling between stones of time.
The vicar's choral, their past love here in the wind's soft breath.
They sang to us that love outlives the change we call death.
There is wisdom in the iris, strength in their long green leaves,
Scent form the clump of honeysuckle, a fragrance in the breeze.

There is music in the nature of this garden, the harp,
Songs of Christian love and flowing themes.
The passage beckons me on.
Do I hear the tramp of Cromwell's men?
Their boots so tread then cease,
Or the whispers of St Thomas, his pensive moods of peace?

The College Gardens
I stop. I sense a change, an open door, the light breaks through.
There, three trusting trees their planting new to Nature's book.
A metal garden gate, open wide, unlocked and unbound,
An escape in time, an expectation, a chord, a sound.
The cottage hollyhock, a purity, with lavender winter-white,
Free-flowering heads of dark red fuchsias, colour blushing bright.
The smile of a velvet flower, a blue surprise,
Laugher in her face, a peeping pansy forever wise.
Here a warmth in the sun's warm kiss with nature blends,
A fading clematis, red-leafed dahlias, strong, stiff and true.
A raised bed of herbs, free-flowering fennel, a yellow musty hue.
A new creation upon a slope overlooking the peaceful waters of
                                        the Wye,
A wisp of bonfire smoke meandering upwards to the bright blue sky.
Standing, I see a myriad of filtered rays dancing midst old
                                        apple trees.
Man's pile of broken sticks, here insects hide, safe to bide.
In this green garden spiritual roots entwine with nature's joy.
A tender yellow poppy, flower of Wales, signifying her wish
                                        for peace.
Change, happy blossom. I feel a mood of human hope.
Sunkissed apples fall, a thrush sings on the Reverend's apple bough,
His warbling songs of love, nature's gift he does endow.
Dreams adrift of poppies pink and poppies red,
A people's mood of modern fantasy, a ballet sown from seed.
The corn marigold, larkspur, red flax, to name but a few,
Each flower belongs. Butterflies flutter one-to-one,
A wasp, a fly, a buzzing bumblebee, all belong.
Oh flowers, buds and bees, I adore you; wild, free and fun.
Summer will fade and Nature's brush will paint the autumn scene.
These gardens set amidst the cathedra's crown to destinies blend.
Garden flowers grow to the light. God is our beacon, our living sun.
I turn to go – smiling. I know the gardener's care will move the
                                        coming dial.

Grace Anderson

CLEETHORPES SEA WALL

Along the sea wall and down by the Marron grass
A carpet of orchids is spread –
Purple and green and extremely beautiful –
mind where you walk – mind where you tread.

Behind there is Buckthorn with berries of orange –
clearly to be seen
Food for the birds in the cold of the winter –
remembering spring that has been.

On the lake behind the wildlife is teeming
Mallard and swan and teal
Six baby ducklings we spied last Wednesday –
out for a swim and a meal.
So if you ever visit our seaside town
and walk along the prom –
Go a bit further away the centre –
look for these treasures –
no matter where you come from.

Maureen Oglesby

LINCOLNSHIRE

On the sunrise ridge were Norsemen strode
And legions gazed I watch the unfurl
Of sky unlimited as through the corntide
Giants walk unbowed by Heaven.

From fishroad to eelslide river,
Guided by quaking alder spires,
The clockmakers of the universe
Rebuilt the world from a violet's leaf.

Bishop and poets called it home.
Moonsteps beyond the man shaped fen
Released God's words to soar and then
Poachers and ploughmen made it home.

This belly of England, carved from wold chalk
By butterfly blue wings, unfolds
Beneath me in a mist of green and sky,
Broader than a poet's dream, crowds heaven around us.

Howard Hewson

POOLSBROOK VILLAGE

An explosion of colour fills my mind
Taking me over to another time
When there was warmth and happiness of a special kind

Passing the farm, milk churns at the ready
Smiling faces of the people keeping the horses steady

Down my old street the evening balmy and alive
With the bustle of families as new babies arrive
Mrs Griffiths helping anyone through life's up and downs
Her presence like the mortar in the bricks of our town

I come to my old house, down the path in a dream
As I step through the door smiles are wide in a welcoming beam
To see me coming home from my travels and trials
Arms enfold me full of loving thoughts which fill the heart of a child
Uncle Harry, Grandma, Grandad and Mum and Dad
Beautiful memories the best I've ever had

The stairs held a secret lobby underneath
Where I hid from the air raids amid the rattle and creaks
As blackout curtains were closed as a sign of the times
Dick Barton on the radio soothed our troubled minds
It was rations and gas masks and privileges few
But happy times yes, not just me and you

Through the door I drift with a sad goodbye
I'll try not to let my loved ones see me cry
Wandering form the Crescent and up to the road
My steps are slow carrying this heavy load
But my mind clears as I return to Poolsbrook Park
The birds are singing and nodding flowers
Bring a welcome lightness to my heart

The lake is sparkling with diamonds from the sky
White swans imperious to all who go by
From my past reflections to this here and now
Precious families bestow a gracious crown

The past and the present are rolled into one
We are on a journey that has only just begun.

Julia Haywood

HOOD WINKING

We once did have a gentle man
Whose name was Robin Hood
And whatever he did do in life
It was all for the good
That is what is told us
As history comes to light
And meetings with our sheriff
It seems a constant fight
What did really happen
Are things which we don't know
For Robin's ammunition
Was an arrow and a bow
We're told the old, old stories
Maybe trouble in the Glen
With Robin and his partners
And the sheriff and his men
Yesterdays get muddled
As more stories do enfold
If true they are so precious
Like finding hidden gold
Gold does not get rusty
So Robin's story glows
Getting better every time
When told by one who knows.

Roy Harvey

THE BEAUTIFUL HIGH PEAK

With moors of purple heather
And rolling hills and peaks,
Rose pink skies at sunset
Turning coral before it sleeps.

Then silver stars shine out at night
Alighting darkened skies,
Illuminating our valleys,
Awakening the owl's cries.

In the early misty morning
As the sunshine warms all things
The mist above the river will rise
To reveal the flash of blue kingfisher's wings.

Like a diamond shining tiara
Rivers flow by soft bending grass
Through meadows of emerald shadows
The mice and small animals pass.

The mighty oak and sycamore
Their branches laden with leaves
Move like huge green clouds of canopy
In the lofty summer breeze.

Even the rain enhances our world
Dewy drops sparkle over it all
Then autumn turns green into gold again
And in winter the wonderland falls.

Shirley Williamson

EXPLORING A BRIGHT COUNTRYSIDE

Walking through the most beautiful countryside
Seeing animals, flowers and artists painting away
Allows me to explore a wonderful walk on my own
This allows me to look at culture

Artists are painting animals and sceneries with flowers
The wildlife are mixing together without any harm
The flowers around are colourful and fresh

While walking through the countryside
I am prepared to take photographs of the area
Including the wildlife, and the colourful flowers around
I am willing to chat with local artists share ideas and explore
                                        their paintings

Later I continue to walk further down the countryside
Where I pass posh cottages with big gardens
They are very bright in colour surrounding with beautiful flowers

Further down, while walking through the countryside
I pass some people picking fresh fruit from a local farm
They are picking strawberries and blackberries
What a great day with plenty of sunshine
The sky is bright pale blue
And there is plenty of fresh air.

Tom Brealey

CHESTERFIELD

Our town has a crooked spire
To see it you will be inspired
Inside is nice and bright
Outside is covered in lights
People come for miles around
To hear the bells a wonderful sound
We have market stalls galore
Food, clothes, pot, pans and more
People come from near and far
The crooked spire is our shining star
I'm proud to say this is my town
It's the best for miles around.

E Riggott

RETURN TO THE RIVER

I remember when the lane was a sheet of ice;
The birds didn't sing along the path to the Pits;
When the presence of Maurice impressed itself on my wits
And I eternised him in poetry.

The birds get used to their new water world;
Lagoons as far as the eye can see;
The Ouse, that bearer of many a dream
Has overflowed. And that, you may say, mightily.

The birds are restless in the Spinney;
They have lost their hunting ground;
But up on a branch, a midget of the species
Trills undaunted. What a rapturous sound!

On the margins hover swans and geese
Seemingly filled with a new unease.
This is not the River they knew:
Now, on the opposite bank, nary a sign of a sheep or a cow.
The water rules! Where to hire a dhow?
The Ouse is everyone's master now!

Tony Sainsbury

LIFE IN FAST LANES

Here in our mountain greenery –
    we have magnificent scenery.
Biker visitors from across the Irish Sea
    come by ferry in June for our Manx TT
Island Tourist Trophy races,
    when fast machines are put through their paces –
Whilst road closures restrict
    our normal pace of life –
We trust that weather conditions
    will not bring strife.
The spectacle of yellow gorse and purple heathers,
    and bikers' leathers, in striking colour, all combine
To set the breathtaking sporting holiday scene for
many spectators
    come and breathe with them the sweet mountain air!

Shireen Markham

BIRTH PLACE

You can never tell when you're young
And life has first begun –
The fondness, your heart will forever hold
For the place of your birth.

And while the years may pass
And the hand of age, – its shadow cast
To that same place –
Your memories will forever belong.

And like the chorus at dawn
And the call of birdsong
In your heart it will remain always
As a place – second to none.

And as the clock of life
Strikes its final chime,
And just as you came
Then so – you're gone.

To all there's no greater place – on this Earth –
Than that of your birth
Of which to, you truly belong.

Bakewell Burt

MAKING HAY IN PANDYR' CAPEL

H eaving lungs, hay feverish, watery eyes,
A s asthmatic curses, reveal the hayseed's rustic charms
Y ouths in hayfields, under blazing cloudless skies
W ith itchy, hay-mottled, sunburnt arms
I n the evening, the haymakers drunkenly dance the 'hay'
R emains of the hay box, now eaten away as . . .
E vening beckons, to make hay of the day.

Jeremy Bloomfield

The Iron Horse Of Merthyr Tydfil

In the year 1804, a man came from Cornwall to Merthyr
of course,
He built the first steam locomotive which was known as 'The Iron Horse'.

Richard Trevithick was his name, forget him we never will,
With a street and gardens, named after him, his memory lives on with us still.

There's a permanent memorial at the top end of town to a very important man,
So why not step on a train and visit us to see where it all began.

Barbara Fowler

Grantham Town

Grantham town in a valley lies with hills on every side
A lofty steeple rising high can be seen from far and wide.
In former days a rural town with a large exquisite church
And an inn with a living beehive sign, river banks with silver birch.
There's a medieval hotel, 'The Angel' it is called
Where kings and queens in centuries past have stayed within
its walls.
There's the school where Isaac Newton want – force of gravity
he found
Film stars and Prime Minister have lived on Grantham ground.
Through two World Wars, devastating Blitz when many lost
their lives
The folk of Grantham soldiered on, survived the wars with pride.
The 'Bouncing Bomb' was created here in St Vincent's stately halls.
The River Witham flows through the parks enhanced
with waterfalls.
It's a busy industrial town right now with increased population
With supermarkets, skate-board park and sports for recreation.

Enid Hewitt

SOUTH HOLLAND, LINCOLNSHIRE

Slowly cutting into the Fens, the rattling train unreels
itself along the lines. It's all sky and little land here,
foreshortening and levelling the plane; a shift of
perspective, all wrenched down to ground level,
then stretched for mile after mile. Slanting rain
hides the distance and it's all liquid now,
horizontal and vertical, leading to the inevitable sea.
Stretched out tight and smooth the bed quilt fields,
stitched with watershine, reach and touch the
ravenous waves that once bit inland. Men still
struggle here to save something, wrest a life.
Otherwhere hedges and rambling dry-stone walls
mark the boundaries. Here drains and mud murky
dykes are frontiers that network the flatter than flat land.
On the map a lattice of thin blue lines shows water
still rules, but it's new-claimed earth locked in by
untrustworthy arteries that might burst full, flood
and retake. Bleak winters on far-flung farms and in tiny
hamlets. Life lonely here, a place to contemplate God
and wrestle demons. The divine felt close but not loving
to the pious, stern people that fled Boston to brave
the ocean and plough a new land. Harsh days, dour
folk, a history of abstinence and life whittled
to the bone. Grey needle spires point to Heaven,
exclamation marks of faith and hope struggling
on through generations. Harsh land, sour soil then,
now drained, reclaimed, flourishing in the blazon *Or*
of rape-seed, surrounded by a field *Vert*.
And approaching Spalding, sun breaks, blazes
gold and green on the chequerboard field-scape.

Keith Linley

DUXFORD (DUKE'S FORD)

I relax, a calm takes over my mind turning off the 505,
it becomes a special place
The ancient souls of Duxford past lie buried
in St Peter's and St John's
Listening for the whistle,
time for playtime to end that look on every child's face
The meeting room of the URC
 holds memories and thoughts of folk long gone

Hurricanes and Spitfires compete
with birds across the grey skies, the birds escape
A church spire nestles inbetween the bright green lime
and flowing willow trees
There in this flat, windy corner of England
with its inspiring sunsets and skyscape
A thatched cottage partly hidden on the village green,
the lanes where you can walk with ease.

Did Kinglsley write 'The Water Babies'
at Duxford Mill (or so I'm told)
Tales told of the American pilots
and football matches and dances
Robbinetts dance hall now just a flint wall
left standing so broken and old
The old school house, the post office
where you take your chances.

June Witt

SEASONS

Spring is alive with activity abounding
All we see is so astounding
Hedges and woodlands have a gorgeous display
Bluebells, primroses and violets all day
We cannot help but be spellbound
The birds' voices too, give us a wonderful sound
Starlings are an amazing sight
As they swirl about in the evening light
Sheep have their lambs, jumping and thriving
While cows with their calves are content in lying.

It is summer with a kaleidoscope of colour
The beauty of the flowers complement each other
Bees are busy on the flowers
Making the most of their great powers
Honey is taken from the hives
They will make more, for their own lives
Crops have grown, from the springtime sowing
Harvesters and trailers, keep the farmers going
Making the patchwork fields a different texture
While the inmates of them are such a mixture
Meadows left wild, are so important to care
For beautiful flowers, butterflies and insects so rare
Farmers now are helped to understand
The plight of our wildlife and give a hand with the land
I reflect upon the summer
The widespread vista of splendid colour.

Pamela Watterson

THE COMEOVER'S WARNING

Wherever you may come from or wherever you have been
I'd like to tell you of the fairest place I've ever seen.
It's hidden in the Irish Sea and keeps its secret well,
But should you ever visit you will fall beneath its spell.
It is, of course, the Isle of Man where fact and legend meet;
Where you will find the pace of life takes on a slower beat.
No inter-city railways or motorways of course,
But just a gentle tram ride where the engine is a horse.

Electric trams and old steam trains are sure to give a thrill;
A legacy from long ago but they are working still.
From water-wheels to castles or from theatre to mines,
Or tholtans on the hillsides almost hidden in the pines;
Whichever way you wander there is such a lot to see.
There's so much on the island that is steeped in history.
The beauty of the landscape is a sight beyond compare
And 'traa dy liooar' or 'time enough' is
uttered everywhere.

I've walked the coast and hillsides but I still remember when
I first encountered magic in a small, secluded glen.
The 'little folk' entrap you as they play beneath the palms.
The Vikings, Celts and many more have fallen for their charms.
So if you come, *you have been warned!* Just be prepared
to stay.
It isn't quite so easy when you try to get away!
I came, I saw, I settled here. That's why I'm so elated.
It only takes one visit to become eManxipated!

Dennis Turner

NOTTINGHAM CASTLE

What's that up yonder
At top of the hill?
Why it's Nottingham Castle
As though time has stopped still.

The mighty statue
Of Robin Hood
Stands nearby.

Ye olde inn
The Trip to Jerusalem
Is at the bottom
Set into the caves.
Folk still drink there
Ale is still sold
Like when the soldiers
Returned from the Crusades
Many tale was told

Hi, time stops still
When you look up yonder
To top of the hill.

Patricia B

THE COAST OF WALES

Here in Wales we live by the sea,
Now it's just my husband and me.
The beach is lovely on a fine day,
When all the children come to play.
Sandcastles and kites and surfboards too,
Walking, running – plenty to do.
Sadly the weather isn't always the best,
But then it's a pleasure to stop for a rest.
The coastal path is a must for the fit,
Walk it all – or maybe a bit.
Wales is varied, that much is true,
A piece of heaven for me and for you.

Josephine Miles

THE WELSH COAST

Listen to the rhythm of the sea
It brings comfort
The waves crashing
The quiet ebb and flow
The waves build so slow
The ocean so clear and blue
Ripples
Sand of glittering gold
Boats bomb on each passing wave
Ozone hangs eerily in the air
It's a flat calm
A soft and gentle motion from the ocean
Make the most of the coast
Take a walk along the Welsh coastline
The vast ocean so blue
Wales will capture you.

Samantha Groves

THEIR LOVELY OLD TOWN

As they look out at their old town
You see the oldies grimace and frown
They mutter and moan, 'It's not the same as it used to be
Our lovely old town that stands by the sea.'

The incomers, newcomers and young don't care
If their old town falls into disrepair
Community spirit is there no more
As generations come and generations go.

The beautiful beaches are fouled by dogs
Their woods have been chopped and used for logs
The time has come they no longer know
Who or what lives next door.

It's a fact, time does not stand still
Changes come, they always will
Never mind to the oldies, it always will be
Their lovely old town that stands by the sea.

Rosaline Jones

MY MOUNTAIN HOME

The tall vibrant fuchsia pink foxgloves grow
In clusters against the dry stone wall.
Waving ferns smother the mountain. Flow
In abundance, compete with stinging nettles yellow gorse.
Purple periwinkle spreads beyond a rocky outcrop,
Climbing the steep slope, I have to stop.
Catch my breath, pause to survey the view.
From this high vantage point, Birds call,
Curlews swoop, cry out, thrushes sing anew.

On this heavenly summer day, sparkling
Blue sea surrounds the rugged coastline of Holy Island.
Yachts glint white in a balmy bay.
I change direction, descend the purple heather slopes.
I reach the winding path to my cottage.
It's hidden among a mass of green treetops,
Sycamores that, left undisturbed by Man
Have seed, spread in abundance in autumn mists.
When the mountain is mellow with black or red berries,
The ferns have turned golden, orangy brown.
In winter, the gales arrive straight off the stormy sea.
Thick mists descend, swirl over the cottage
To drench the dying garden of flowers
And leave stark skeletons of bare branches
Once, we had a heavy snowfall.
It fell silently all day and night,
Until the magical moon appeared all crystal white.
The driven snow bathed frosty garlands on tree branches.
A red robin looked for scraps,
Loitered around the doorstep to wait.
A badger had left his footprints across the garden by the gate
Before crossing the virgin track to his den.
I suddenly felt alone now my husband had died.
He too, would have loved this winter scene.
It stays cold until spring arrives, snowdrops
Heralding daffodils, tulips, new shrubs.
Holyhead Mountain is alive with new growth.
A collage of shades, lilacs, greens, spiky gorse.
Bluebells bloom in the woodland dell.
Soon swallows arrive to feed in mid-air.
Buzzing bees pollinate the spring flowers.
Life's cycle has begun again in this peaceful paradise.

Jean Charlotte Houghland

ACCURSED MANICHEANS IN BLAENAU GWENT

No 'Gwledig'
Territorial leader
Answers to education
Does Wales lie under curse?

Facebook, Twitter, are they discipline?
Reminds me a personal active nobody
Self-revealing singular selfish cruelty
Assembly members fiddle like Nero

How on Earth does one
Allow oneself to write like this?
In uncomfortable company
One or two easily killed

Dark tunnels of uncertainty
Gwalia Deserts
Education virtues of themselves
Turned into terrible vices

Thinking like this
One forms 'Symbol'
Detect false dual 'Simulacra'
Wales no heritage or reality

Think about the children of Wales
Vernon Watkins, Idris Davies, dear David Jones
Education now a deserted citadel
The least I can do is protest

General tepidity listless parents
Marxist reification is back
Free after morning pills
Answer to child experiments

Do we have anonymous atheists close to God?
Anonymous Christians closer to atheism?
Beaufort choir sings in hope
Who pays the 'Ferryman' to Hades?

Paul Faulkner

LAND OF OUR FOSTERFATHERS

This land of Druids, dreamers, sages, saints, friends,
Music, poetry, dancing and delight,
Where the veil seems thin, hiding Heaven's realm,
This land, generous as ever,
Nurtured two souls, as teenage incomers,
Still safely oversees their earthly ends.

Twin souls apart by fifteen years and many miles,
Singly found faith and freedom here in Wales,
Majesty in mountains, rivers, woodlands,
Waterfalls and stunning land and seascapes.

He at fifteen fled the stiff upper lip
Of frigid fashionable Folkestone
For warmth and safety from the threat of war
In motherly Merthyr's gentleness and calm,
For Cyfartha Castle's academia
With spiritual sanctuary in chapel sermons
And fellowship at last with teenage peers.

She, the lucky lass from Lancashire,
Knew family fun and games in Anglesey,
Caravan, carnivals, helping with harvest,
Galloping gleefully over the beaches,
Joyfully jumping the waves and swimming,
Even on horseback, in the rough, clean sea,
And scrambling barefoot over craggy rocks,
Laughing and playing on the sunny sand,
While all the rest of Britain moped in rain.

Later gains a liberal education,
Through scholarship, to good St Winifred,
Sang in choir, acted Shakespeare – and the fool!
Served in chapel, swept the dorm, learned to live
In Christian community . . . microcosm?
Saw sunsets over sparkling Menai Straits –
Magic and mystery. Was the Virgin ever here
At Llanfairfechan . . . Church of Mary by the stream?

Much later, much older, memories rife,
Needing rest, recreation and fun,
We came again, for playing and paddling,
To Anglesey to rediscover joy,
And find it, magically, in Moelfre,
By sun and moonlight on the silent sea.
Then in golden years to Craig Fawr. Sunshine
In February and resolve to move for good.

Whitford with St Beuno and St Mary's:
Walking with friends, the 'Whitford Wanderers',
Fun with fellowship and family joy,
Mertyn Downing, Thomas Pennant's once,
Ours for the happiest of happy times.
Weddings, christenings of our first grandchild.

Facing up to failing powers, moving
Mournfully to Yr Wyddgrug, Mold.
(Yr Wyddgrug, sadly means a burial place)
Theatr Clwd as a special treat!
Comfort of Moel Famau, 'Mummy Mountain',
And yes, a new beginning for us both.

New languages: Polish and signing
With the Deaf Christian community,
Then to St Mary's – Margaret Beaufort's,
History, beauty, tradition and calm;
Ecumenism, with multi-faith friends –
Made a magazine called 'Ever Wondered?'

Nearby Wrexham . . . forty-eight languages spoken . . .
Llangollen . . . Eisteddfod, harmony, unity,
Tangnefedd, deep peace, highest ideals.
Dreams of a World without any fighting,
Ever wondering at the beauty all around,
In nature and all beings . . . even human!

For blessings to minds, hearts, senses, spirits,
For a final, kindly, gentle, helping hand,
For 'Croeso y Cymru', Diolch yn fawr,
Beloved Wales, our fostermotherland

Jill V Clark

WHISPERING, 'YOU'VE MADE IT'

Commanding view over Newport, Risca, Cwmbran in
South Wales
A Gwent region landmark, Twm Barlwm mountain lies, with silent tales
On a clear day, from the top to see panoramic view of the Bristol Channel
Reach the height after trekking, exercise, cool forehead a watered flannel
Climbing past rock remains, Iron Age hill fort, near to the summit
Built by Celts during Roman times, warriors whispering, 'You've made it'

A place to aim for, mainly to sit and stare, a local treasure
It rises up 1375 feet hands to assist the climber, distance
to measure
Leading into hill and mountain, countryside wild with grass trails
Past broken rock, weathered woodland, waving at the wind, like sails
Swooping birds fly high, lack of grazing, makes an empty
wild picture
Seen for miles around, with the pimple on top, a
permanent fixture

Walking or running brings the strength of legs tightening
and stretching
Fair game for those with pen and paper needed for sketching
At the top those who sit on rocks engage in reflecting, stocktaking
Time to eat sandwiches, drink coffee, prepared before,
in their making
Trekking to Cwmcarn Drive, the forest verdant, an industry of walks
Where reception and coffee rooms dwell and centre guides give talks

Brace the wind for fierce it feel around the legs, blowing away the hair
The howling whistling noise, a thunderous voice, grabbing
to tear
Through earth's feet, sound breaking 'mountain organ' unsettling, raw
Experience gusting wind touching all parts of the body to paw
It tells of this naked power, here to stay, when humans
have gone
Before and after in time, everlasting for the duration and strong

The wind sound is best heard at the southern slope of the hill
Set out from here along Gwent ridge if weather-beaten walker has the will
Or come down the way you came, where ghosts of Celtic tribes stand out
Faster past ancestors of Iron Age fort, who again challenge with a shout
Or join others, who on Good Friday climb as pilgrims,
mountain assault
Today's motorbikes that hinder should beware old warriors that cry, 'Halt.'

Ron Constant

LLANDUDNO

Summertime is here again
Tho' I'll take my umbrella
For it may rain.
We are off to the place
Where we love to go
The seaside resort of Llandudno.

As we walk from the prom
To the Victorian pier
As you listen out, you may clearly hear
Speedboats cruising through the sea
As we watch over, with a nice cup of tea.

Seagulls passing over our head
As they search and hunt for crumbs and bread
Gazing over the mountain Orm
Looks like there could be a storm

So it looks like it's time
For us to go,
But we will be back before you know
To the place where we always go
The seaside resort of great Llandudno.

Susan Rance

THE TOWY VALLEY

In the autumn sunlight
We watched a fine buck
Resting in the bracken.

Only a noble crown of antlers
Appeared above his misting breath.
Beside the giant holmoak grazed
A dozen contented does,
Untroubled by the raven's
Passing croak.

A reason for their enduring peace?
It could be the end of the
Rutting season.

Robert Wynn-Davies

ARTHUR'S STONE

In January rain, unceasing and grey,
hanging over the land,
wrapping, enfolding the day,
I came to Arthur's Stone.
To Maen Ceti, the chambered tomb,
unmoved and solitary on the brown hill.
Sick and sleepless, with a mind needing room
in which to grow the next ten years.
It is here that some mystery,
beyond knowledge, beyond memory and history,
has split, sliced a slab from the capstone.
Burning, magnetic, the cold wetness of the megalith
crawled under my touch as I waited alone.
Under my hand in the rain I felt it lurch,
the hill, the peninsula, island and planet.
Wet-footed and calm, I went home from my search
Without fact, without enlightenment or truth,
With only the secret of feeling.

Anthony James

BEACH MEMORIES – TENBY

The beach is open and wide
The soft sand is right by your side
The wonderful memories
Memories of Tenby Beach
Is such a great feeling inside
It's such a beautiful place
Where I used to go as a child
Even now it's still great
With all the wonderful
The wonderful memories inside
Tenby beach is the true place to go
To have that great feeling inside.

Angela Cole

THE COLLIER'S SPIRIT

For Dad (Harold Frowen) and Grampa (Arthur David Thomas)

The day awakes to the pit's siren
calling men and boys from slumber to her bosom
stealing them away from the warmth of loved ones
and they answer the call wearily with the
echo of hob-nailed boots on cobbled stone
winding their way toward the pit wheel
serving as a giant compass in the early morning sky
leading them to the cold, damp, dark and dusty pit
if they had a choice they would go in another direction
any direction other than the depths of that pit
and they joke and sing quelling the fear
knowing that this could be their last glimpse of the day
before being swallowed in the pit's hunger
keeping them locked forever in her dark embrace
where she fails to crush
the collier's spirit
for it will never be broken or die
as it burns brightly as their lamps once did
in the hearts of those they loved
and left behind.

Jan Maissen

SOUTHSEA

My mam she was a Welsh girl
My dad from Dewsbury
Got married in a church nearby
And settled in Southsea.

They had two sons and two daughters
One daughter, that is me
And I will never wander
From this village called Southsea.

It's just outside of Wrexham
Just two miles maybe three
And at the end of every day
That's where I'm going to be.

Post office and hairdressers
And Forge Road surgery
We've even got a pub right her
To quench our thirst you see.

And just like me, my husband
He was brought up in Southsea
Like the ex-mayor of Wrexham town
Who lives a few doors up from me.

In Southsea there's a river
It never fails to be
We local folk all know it by
The 'Reddy' in Southsea.

The slacky bank has changed now
But we can still recall
The happy times we played there
When we were only small.

We used to have a poet
Her name was Marjorie
But now she's buried with my dad
In All Saints church, Southsea.

Carol Rance

THE ANGLESEY STEAM RALLY

We have just been to a steam rally.
It's a place where people seem pally.
There were stalls with linens and threads,
other selling plants for nursery beds.
Junk stalls with some bric-a-brac finds.
Marquees displaying crafts of all kinds.
Puffing engines with happy proud owners,
very interesting even to loners.
There were cars from bygone ages,
couldn't be bought now from small wages.
Stationary engines all chugging along,
motorbikes that were bought for a song.
All owners with dusters to clean
precious exhibits, a joy to be seen.
Fairground organs playing a tune,
The wonderful day was over too soon.
Ice cream wagons still called us out,
calories were forgotten no doubt.
Last of the goods were being sold,
sun went in, it was turning cold.
What a great weekend we all had,
clearing away, no time to be sad.

Ann May Wallace

SWANSEA TODAY

Swansea today,
Has come a long way.
Once a mining scene.
Now portrayed on a TV screen.
The breeze of the Mumble's air.
To see the Apple shape shop there.
The pier stands alone.
And Swansea Market for a tea and scone.
The Quadrant is a hive of activity.
And travels of Dr Who add complexity.
From New Earth to West Germany.
It has all been filmed in this city.

Peter Evans

MY VALLEY

I love my valley so green,
High mountains surround it,
So tall and serene,
Horses gallop wild and free
A lovely sight for walkers to see
Purple winberries everywhere,
Staining hands and feet but
I don't care!
Over the mountain not far away
A beautiful castle, once owned by Crawshay,
A hard cruel man who ruled with an iron rod,
On his wife's grave is 'Please forgive him God'
The black gold men dug from the ground
Put their hearts into music for a beautiful sound,
So many things I'd like to say
Please forgive me I pray
I will write some more another day.

Maureen Margaret Thornton

THANK GOD

Thank God for here
in a summer like this

Lord
keep me from Rayner's Lane.
Eastcote. Pinner.
Going back again
to the death in life
commute by train.
And Northwood Hills.
Which exists.
Still.

John Judd

GREENFIELD VALLEY HERITAGE PARK

Once, in this place, beneath the trees,
The water fell from pool to pool
To feed the needs of industry.
And here on these paths, through grassy banks,
Small children trudged from day to day,
To serve the needs of industry.
While here in this clearing, stood the mill,
Where children toiled from dawn till dusk,
To meet the needs of industry.
And this is the road the children climbed,
To give thanks for their daily bread,
And a day of rest from industry.

But now, in this place, beneath the trees,
The little children skip and run
Along the paths, through grassy banks,
And pause to rest among wildflowers,
Where butterflies dance over crumbling stones
And tumbling streams and waterwheels,
That turn no more for industry.

Then off they go to feed the ducks
And clap their hands at squabbling geese,
Or gaze perhaps, at stately swans
That glide across the silent pools.

This is the place beneath the trees,
Where children come to play;
A verdant valley, where nature bears,
A testament to childhood.

Joan Conway

MY VIEW

The evening sun sets behind the vast silent hills of our
Celtic mystery
An ancient castle surrounded by mist steeped in centuries' history
Deep amongst purple heather lies the truth of King
Arthur's stone
This legend belongs to the earth, wild mountain ponies
free to roam.

A lonely cast iron lighthouse stands, gazes before my
eyes so strong
Landmark for generations meet horizons where the open
seas belong
Galleons fallen deep, golden treasures show their face on secluded coves
The haunted, smuggling rector knocks at night, on a deserted rectory door.

In the distance an island of dedicated, faithful monks bow, keel and pray
Solitary with God, contented, their simple daily life the Cistercian way
Cockle pickers dig, back the breaking task, hoping for a
decent hoard
Carefully tread on sinking sand, watching clouds as claps of thunder roar.

Seagulls squawk, perfect angelic wings blanket over mackerel skies
Trawlers, skiffs, sail at dusk, searching for a catch on a neap tide
Creeping seaweed covers rocks, leading into dark illusions
of caves
Storms of rolling surf, innocent grey Atlantic seals fight
the waves.

Sure-footed sheep cling to cliff edges, tranquil, oblivious
to any fear
Lost mariners washed up from wrecks, their souls lie deep in graves near
Ruined holy chapels buried, leaving footprints of saints on headland at sea
My world is the ever-failing ocean, its landscape and beauty stare at me.

Long tall grasses waver in the wind, as the delicate sea
lavender blows
Nature is wonderful, complete, peace and harmony it
quietly grows
An artist's masterpiece to view each day, I could not ask for any more
How privileged I am to dwell, where the land meets the rippling shore.

Anne Williams

100

THE LEE CLUB

There's Molly and Shirley
Leslie and Rachel E. (nee Kelly)
Sitting round a table
Telling poems and fable
Drinking coffee or Rosie Lee.

We are artists and able,
Steady and stable
And won't entertain ugly,
We are a Lee club not a Glee club
And our aim is to see beauty.

We go to Llanover Hall
An arts centre for all
A national treasure
Its price beyond measure,
But if your name ends in 'ohn, 'er or 'oan
You will have to be in a club of your own!

Rachel E Joyce

RHOSSILI

I gaze upon an enchanting scene
Where the hills are dressed in shades of green.
The rugged rocks stand high with pride,
Beneath the rocks is the calling tide,
Where surfers come to seek a ride,
And visitors come from far and wide
Gliders take off from the hilltops high,
Enjoying the beauty from the sky.
The sandy beach is so fresh and clean,
Making this an idyllic scene.
Her beauty no one can compare,
We must look after her with care
Giving her our best respect,
Embracing lovingly without neglect.
She has other sisters around the coast,
Although it's not for me to boast.
But visit them and you will see,
Why my favourite place is Rhossili.

L J Dhar

A School Visit To Caerphilly Castle

Wide-eyed in wonder,
I cross to the gate.
To enter the giant,
The past to relate.
Its giant walls invite me,
To cross to the past.
Its stones are so mighty,
They were built to last.
It's just like a monster,
Lying asleep.
The bastions and towers,
Its sentinel keep.
Shadows confront me,
As I enter within.
The cold wind of history,
And the battles begin.
I hear once again,
The arrows in flight,
And a hand grips my heart,
As the ghosts walk at night.
I want to explore every turret I see,
But the shadows are frightening,
And the past lives through me.
My heart races madly,
As I see in the hall,
The ghosts at their dancing,
As they slip through the wall.
A hand on my shoulder,
A step that's so slow,
And teachers beside me.
It's time that we go.

Gwyneth Pritchard

SANDY BAY

Welsh summer days,
Still, spirits raise!
They cannot take away,
Loved Sandy Bay.
Sea breeze, the beach, warm sands,
Those childhood lands.
We knew the harebells fairy blue.
Dew-foot, the golden gorse,
Lone-rider and white horse.
The ebb and flow of tides,
To seek, the crab who hides,
A limpet on a string.
Then up we'd bring!
Loved holidays,
Where childhood stays.
Grey rocks to run,
Hot-samfire scent the sun.
Without a care,
God's Heaven near!
When simple pleasures were.
Tea on the beach,
A donkey ride,
And visits to the fair!

Ann E Doney

OGMORE CASTLE AT SUNSET

My shadow touches stepping stones,
The Ogmore river slipping between
Like dark tongues on grey teeth
Towards the graveled bank,
Below the castle's granite hand.

Those stony-fingered walls
Are honey with the dipping sun;
Broken battlements casting shades
That twist as the evening cowls,
Whilst the river softly murmurs
Its vespers to the sea.

A young couple dressed for summer
Laugh past me to bound onto
The stone's hand in outstretched hand,
Leaping to reach the further bank
Then kiss and wave back to me.

I wave but youth dances on,
Not looking at those proud remains
They run to the dimming farm beyond
And as the tide whispers in
The river shakes the moon.

Robert Bellamy

WHO NEEDS TO GO ABROAD?

Who needs to go abroad when we have Gower?
A beautiful place in sunshine, or shower.
So near the sea on every side
With sandy beaches that are long and wide,
Or secluded inlets and secret bays
Reached by lanes, or rutted, twisting, ways
Through old woods of hawthorn trees and ash,
Or grassy dunes with flowers along the path.
Old farms and churches from years gone by
On hilly rises or in valleys lie.
Hidden villages, a few houses, or more,
Among woods and fields, or above the shore.
Cefn Bryn, its ridge of ferns and heather
Bathed in sun, or battered by rough weather,
Has north/south views to take the breath away
Towards distant hills, over sea and bay.
High above the estuary's mouth
Rises Llanmadoc Hill, facing south
Towards Rhossili, the gem in the crown,
Stretching for miles beyond Harding's Down.
Not the only jewel, for there's Whitford beach
Remoter, lonely, far out of reach.
Miles of dunes with their forestry trees,
And the distant lighthouse braving the seas.
Who needs to go abroad? Not me, no way,
When I can go to Gower to spend the day!

Haidee Williams

THE OAK TREE

O might oak
So tall and strong
You stand the test
Of time
You witness all
And yet remain
A statue so sublime

Your canopy has sheltered
And Protected
Man and beast
Your roots are anchored
In the earth
Your fruit a squirrel's feast

Once you numbered
In your millions
Cut down
To build tall ships
In many forms
You sustained our lives
And helped us to exist

Nothing lasts forever
But you a tree remain
A tall and strong example
Of all that is not vain.

Ron Houghton

ANGEL COVE

Grey seals stretch, on stony sandy shore.
Gulls dive, whirr, cries penetrate thin air.
Hues of variegated colour; sunbeams smile and yawn.
My soul consumed, inflamed, reborn.

I clamber down towards the shore,
Full of vigour, eager to explore.
Chrysanthemum-tailed rabbits, ears twitching, all alert,
Playing tug-of-war. Lichen, soft mosses, cushion my feet;
Whilst harebells, rock roses and yarrow slowly retreat.

Seals swim in swirling waters, heads bobbing, turning round.
Peace descends upon the scene and nature makes no sound.
Morning wanes, the sun climbs high, guardian of the azure sky.
Shadowed pools and dappled rocks, humming bees
and dragonfly.

My gaze averts to high above and I begin to climb.
Nature plays a game; and I am lost in time.
Capricious weather as I reach high ground.
Peace swiftly felled by a raging sound.

Clouds spurt saliva, mocking the sun.
Curling, creamy waves, hit-and-run.
Sand shivers, drawn back and forth;
Violated by wind from the north.
Angel Cove, a wondrous treasure.
Angel Cove, my greatest pleasure.

Carole McKee

BEET FEET

One night I walked along the dunes
and back from Prestatyn to Rhyl.
Full moon shining brightly
but forgot my funny pill.
That's alright no one in sight
not even the Bill.
So scenery I took in warily
at my will.

Passing by the bins
this was my reflection.
Intermittent rubbish bags
tied up for collection.
No dogs in sight or sound.
Down now off the sand dunes
I shortly tread their ground.

Sun Centre like a giant signpost,
stood out in the moonlight
patiently awaiting the crowds
this was a glorious sight.

Tide was in where had it been,
looking round, had I been seen?
No I wasn't hiking, just couldn't sleep,
my thoughts were of my idol, a bit too deep.

Rhyl is where he lives
with memories to keep.
Past the little tear bar where we sat out in the sun
thinking of the friendship and the joy we had to come.
Here I am, there's a light on, I know I should be gone
Back home to Prestatyn to bed
to rest my weary feet and head.

Six or seven yuppies, did they pose a threat?
Don't want to be dead but I'm not home yet.
Arcades dimly lit
but nowhere to place a bet.

About turn past the bowling alley
back onto the prom
fresh air and a warmth
holiday makers not one.

Concrete steps and sand dunes
all the way home
no key so I kipped with the rabbit
in the shed till the rising sun,
then wearily off to work until the day was done.

Rhyl my neighbour, I will savour
and visit again some daytime.
Shopping, sunbathing and visiting friends
On a bus that will save time.

Karen Gilmour

A CWM TOO FAR

It is cool beneath the overhead canopy of leaves
On the walk down Blaen y Cwm to the sea.
Ahead lies the Bristol Channel, innocently serene.
Today, sunbeams dance at her water's edge,
And gulls ride her gentle waves,
But beware the sea with her smiling summer face.
She is as dangerous now as on a winter's day,
When storm-tossed waves cascade over her
Limestone cliffs, hurling pebbles far inland.
The hypnotic rhythm of her endless ebb and flow
Lures the unwary to forget the tides
And walk the sands of Y Traeth Mawr.
Close your ears to her siren call,
For Dunraven is more than a step away,
And danger lurks in this tranquil place.
As the hunter stalks its prey, so she can swiftly turn,
Engulfing the headlands and trapping the foolish,
The iron ladder at Cwm Bach their one hope now.

Patricia McKenna

GLORIOUS DEVON

Brunel's railway hugging the coast
Takes us where we like it the most
Pastures green with rich red loam
Jam and cream upon our scones

Sidmouth, Exmouth and Teignmouth too
Their rivers greeting a sea of blue
All three exude individual charm
Here in a bay filled with summertime warmth

Cockington village – thatched cottages galore
Roses and Hollyhocks surround every door
Torquay's a jewel with sparkling allure
Almost identical to the Cote d' Azur

Palm trees grow here as the climate is fairer
A marvel of England's very own Riviera
Paignton is lovely with its impressive zoo
And it offers us boat trips and steam train rides too

Brixham is interesting – an old working port
We see lots of fish on the quayside being caught
Its harbour, a very safe haven for boats
Sheltering from storms helps to keep them afloat!

Dartmouth's very pretty – it has such natural beauty
Ferries sailing all the while perform essential duty
Here Agatha Christie settled in her home
Inspired to write her novels of very great aplomb

Next we visit Plymouth Sound – not too far to go
Soon we see the splendid sights along the famous Hoe
Strong naval traditions from years of old
Where Francis drake played skillful bowls

This gallant captain with resolute ardour
Set sail from here to defeat the Armada
And pilgrims sailed west to discover new lands
But we're staying put here at Goodrington Sands

Finally to Dartmoor – it truly is amazing
Everywhere around us, little ponies grazing
Windy, harsh and wild it feels
Yet has its own unique appeal

Glorious Devon – a pleasant land
With combe and tor and golden sands
We've so enjoyed our visit and stay
The perfect place for our holidays

Gary K Raynes

TYWYN (GWYNEDD) – MY SLICE OF PARADISE

Gentle waves roll in off a sea suffused with hints of blue
and green.
Each wave ending its long journey with a rush of bubbles
and foam.
The beach of fine golden sand patiently built up by
countless waves.
While the sea itself is touched with a sparkle of foam and shimmer of light.
Inland the frowning peak of Cader Idris presides over
lesser hills.
Then shrouds its head in mist and dark rain-bearing clouds.
This is a gentle green valley that is open to the salt-laden air.
Well-weathered hills that have endured a thousand winters of snow and ice.
Watered by rain, their gentle flanks covered by green fields.
Flowing through the valley the River Dysynni on its way
to the sea.
Eventually losing its identity in the waters of Cardigan Bay.
Its lower waters saline and flowing in and out of a
brackish lagoon.
Home to majestic mute swans gliding on its mirrored
swirling waters.
No famous castle to be seen dominating this quiet valley.
Only the grass grown ruins of Castell-Y-Bere.
Yet sea, valley and mountains combine to create such beauty.
This special place in Wales that is my little slice of paradise.

Keith J Davies

FROM MONMOUTH TO CHEPSTOW BY THE OLD ROAD

Sun gleams through woodland glade.
Gold lines road edges.
Last green leaves cling to the vaults of trees,
Filigree branches arch against the sky
Roots in a froth of rushing bracken.
Blorenge, the Sugar Loaf the skyline;
Old mountains knowing an eternity
Of rain, sun, wind and ice.
Bold against the sky's calm.
The old bus rattles its way along twisting lanes,
Filled with friendship's chatter
Today's glory, yesterday's floods.
Passing the dark of the plough;
Pastures quietly dotted with sheep.
The point of Trellech church
Rises above long ages of love and life,
Peace and war.

Set down,
Feet firmly set in Earth's soil again,
Linking with all creation
In a wonder of loveliness.
In the Earth's turmoil, an oasis.

Margaret Davis

WINTER IDYLLS (SNOWDONIA)

A time to think, when times are still,
Of dreams gone by, dreams to fulfill
The landscape lies a spectre grey
Sleeping through another day.

Deep in the valley, a bell shall toll,
In a place that rests the soul.
Where epitaphs and lovely verses
On slate and stone – reimburses.

Across the moor, flees the frightened doe
As the kestrel hovers to claim its foe.
A silent copse with trees so bare,
Places by nature, with loving care.

Then, as for a thousand years,
The mountains will shed their tears.
Riverlets will start to flow,
Expanded by the melting snow.

Lush green grass, soft and mellow
Sprinkled with bells of yellow.
Lambs will bleat and birds will sing,
Welcome home – O glorious spring!

Raymond Johnson-Hughes

NO SHOES

I'll go the gipsy way, a fair way,
My caravan and I.
Pots and pans, a stove to burn some fuel,
A horse will I have, no mule.

The chilly air I'll taste
But I won't go in haste.
The earth is calling,
My old dog snoring –
I'll go the gipsy way,
I say.

Summer's sweet scents I'll taste,
The clip-clop of my horse's hooves,
I won't need any shoes,
All I'll need is the cold night air
And an owl hooting yonder.

Susan Jane Byers

THE RIVER USK, NEWPORT 2012

Ten years ago, a ship was found
Buried in the mud for many years
On the banks of the River Usk.

Newport was now on the map.
A historical place of renown,
A city now and not a town.

Scholars came from far and wide,
Just like a flowing tide,
To see what had been found
On the banks of the River Usk.

More ships are still buried there
Waiting their turn to be found,
Lying under the thick, cloying mud
Found on the banks of the River Usk.

One day all will see that proud ship
Floating high again on the tide.
No more in the mud, but on the waters
Covering the banks of the River Usk.

John Harrold

TOWN TO CITY

A town – not too pretty
Was suddenly a city
With a status at last
Insignificance was past.
An event in modern history
Written down for all to see.

Nothing much has changed for us,
Town or city, we don't fuss.
A place is memories, not name –
The seaside – a football game.
A train ride that we went on –
'The Mumbles Train' – long, long gone,
The Gower coast – rocks and sea
Snapshots in time for me.

Swansea City or Swansea Town.
Words of history noted down,
Just my home, my haven and rest,
Place and time I love the best.

Judith Jones

THIS LAND OF MINE

When asked, 'Where do you live?'
I give the only answer I can give
'I live on islands guarded by the sea
Living in peace, lucky to be free'
'Yes – but where is this land you've got?
Are you English, Ulster, Welsh or Scot?'
I say, 'I am a member of this British land
In case you do not understand
We here are brothers in our heart
When threatened, I will take my brother's part.'
'Yes, but where born? The place you lay your head?'
I say, 'Just anywhere you see, I'm British born and bred.'

Gordon Andrews

IN THIS PLACE

They asked me why I like this little place –
small, unimportant, just one rambling street,
an ancient castle, half a dozen shops,
a school, a friendly pub, not much to see.

How could I try to make them understand
when they prefer the towns with office blocks,
department stores, all rush and traffic jams?
No sight of sky or stars, just unreal light –
and crowds and crowds of people.

I used to like that too – until I saw
that all the people simply passed me by.
For them it seemed as if I was not there –
like robots, they were programmed just to go
their lonely way, ignoring all the rest,
never having time to smile or speak –
strangers all to one another.

In this place I stroll the single street
and no one passes by without a smile,
a wave, a greeting, some a cosy chat.
There is no rush to get to anywhere,
everyone has time to make me feel
that I'm the person who they wished to meet.
Each desires just to be a friend –
invaluable friends – and they live here.

Now when they ask me why I like this place
I tell them that I love to see the sky,
the well-farmed fields with buildings nestling close,
the quiet wind, and rain upon my face.
But more than this, it's knowing endless joy
experienced by all who come and find
there are no strangers her.

Joan Bell

STRANGER IN A STRANGER LAND

I came to Wales as a stranger in a stranger land
Leaving behind the forest of Yvelines
The garden of my grandmother
Roots of my childhood
Walking barefoot on the sands
The sea shimmering grey and mauve
The colour of inner shells
I heard a voice in my head
Saying: listen with your bones
To the heartbeat of Mother Earth
Pulsing along the ley-lines
Open up to the beauties of this land
Let the wind and the rain bless you
The sun caress you
Let your spirit fly with the buzzards and the crows
Dance for the shy foxes
Dream with the owls
Roll in the grass
Your child within is welcomed
The veil between the worlds
Is so thin in Wales
The fairy land of Tir-nan-Og
Embracing you so tight
One day, my mother told me on the phone
'Do you realise, Sylvie, you have been in Wales for a quarter of a century?'
I didn't see time passing
Dancing my dreams awake
In coves and forest glades
Sidestepping on tiptoe
Through the shadows of the moon
Drinking from the healing wells of Bishopswood
I think I have found the sacred stones
To lay down my weary head
End of my pilgrimage on Earth
In the land of Wales.

Sylvie Alexandre-Nelson

PLEASANT PASTIMES

Historical Margam Castle
Draws people to its park
Orangery is the place
For music concerts and shows
Hidden deer sometimes sighted.
Feeding ducks on the pond
Then to Abbots Kitchen for meals

On Welsh mountains there are ponies
Ambling – in pose
Brecon ponies seldom seen
Crunching fresh green grass
Streams of water flowing
After April's rain.

Where wild flowers flourish
I walked with you
In birth of summer's season
On Baglan Mile End Field.

Mary Hughes

AT THE CAFÉ

There are the two ladies who always stop for a coffee and catch up on gossip
I go in on Saturdays for my big veggie breakfast
Friday morning takeaway veggie sausage and onion rolls
People pass by and look at us through the window
Whatever the weather you can be sure of a welcome from Julia
It's a place to drop in for breakfast or lunch, for coffee or tea
For children or adults or teenagers too, to sit and talk or dream
To send text messages on mobile phones or read a magazine
Sipping a coffee and watching the rain; a friend may see me and call in
I like to try and get in by the window to watch the world go by
To have time to sit and not be hassled to pay up and get out
We all get to know each other and exchange greetings
and chat
In Welsh or English, both languages are spoken
and understood
In the café in Terrace Road in Aberystwyth you will find all that.

Melanie M Burgess

THIS ROMANCE OF WALES

There are many valleys turned into vast lakes that covered
the dales
These rich men buy the countryside, it's goodness they take from Wales
They rob the Welsh nations of its treasures, they ruined
the dales
How could they destroy the beautiful pasturelands of Wales?

This is our heritage, the hearts of the Welsh nation beat
with pride
When we walk the dales and hills of this beautiful countryside
Those ugly pits are now closed down, the hills and the trees grow again
Where once the countryside and the beautiful farmland cried
in pain

The streams and rivers that once flowed black are now fresh and clean
The nightmares are over, the countryside has come thro' its bad dreams
The sweet dales are now newly-born, they planted trees upon the hills
Those quarries that once worked have stopped, the land is quiet and still

Those reservoirs they built this storage place for water have become a boating lake
The countryside and open fields, the beauty has been restored, is now awake
Those small pathways you walk will take you to the heart of
the dales
This beautiful land I have romanced when I fell in love
with Wales

When I leave Wales, please let my body be put in the dales
So my soul will walk the beautiful countryside of Wales
The air plucks my heart like the strings of a harp
The deep love for Wales, the dales, plays every part.

John F Grainger

THE LANDSCAPE

There are times, more frequently these days,
When my mind wanders back to summers long ago.
To the days of open meadows beyond the great elm
Trees I used to play through as a child. All gone now.

As if just yesterday, I still see in my mind's eye
The statuesque pose of the Red Deer there. And the
Elegant, graceful step of his soft-eyed doe, nibbling
In the undergrowth – seemingly indifferent to his Posturings.

I remember each year the first witterings of the
Blue-backed swallows as they swept in from the south
To the Old Water Mill after their long, long flight
From Africa – home again and happy; as was I to
See and hear them always heralding the new Summer.

I recall the lake I used to walk around, and in time
Rowed upon; with the Lilies and Rhododendrons quivering
In the summer breezes. The big fish supposedly in it
Which no one could ever catch – including me.
The reflection of the shimmering sunlight, glistening.
And the *plop* and the ripples emanating after I
Flicked a small stone in for effect – as I always did.

There would be afternoons lying under a copper beach.
Digesting the empyrean blue above and making shapes
Out of the occasional drifting clouds that blundered past, oblivious;
Or feeding Nutty the squirrel and his family – who nimbly
Scurried and scuttered up and down the branches to us for an
Easy meal – always just out of reach. I never did manage to
Get him to take from my hand, though very nearly as I recall:
I am sure.

It seemed the bracken stretched for miles, about waist high.
And somewhere, always in the distance, you could hear the
Gamecock cry. But I was smaller then and periods in which year
These occurred must be a little muddled now – I just recall the
Emotions to the sunshine; and sights and sounds and occasionally
The smells of the memories – fresh, so they must have been in
Summer – I guess.

Life was better then: my Mother and Father alive, brothers, sisters,
My friends – all long since gone: some in war; some in accident
Or illness; and others through the decades as their time was
Finally called – uncheated of their years, like the others.
Each in their different ways, from youth, they enriched my life
And I miss them. Still, in my memories, they are there – forever

The same and in their prime; as I live and breathe – part of me.

I think I said this before – I wish, more frequently
These days, I could travel back to that lost landscape of
My immaturity; wishing to comprehend, now that which I
Accepted unknowingly then: how could I know?
The revelations only come in time, as is the natural process.
Not by inborn prescience.

Yet a reaffirmation of my premature perceptions; of family,
Place, myself, old friends and events would be a suitable
Conclusion. If but nothing else, I think the meaning to
My life is surely found in the comprehension of its
Experience. And with that,
The real beauty of that landscape.

Frank G Dorber

MY HERITAGE

I'll climb to the top of Snowdon
In the early morning dew,
Just to see the panorama
And the unending view.

These hills and rugged mountains
Tranquility all abound,
Is my own little heaven
With peace and silence around.

Silence will sometimes be broken
The screech of a kite on high,
Or a Hawk of a local squadron
As it suddenly flies by.

This realm of magical beauty
Is there for us all to see,
What artist can paint this picture?
And say to you it is free.

Looking down below, I wondered
What Man has made of his land
It cannot compare in any way
To God's own artistic hand.

Clifford Jones

THE GARDEN

Last night I saw a garden, it really caught my eye
There were seagulls on the gateposts
With wings spread out to fly
But never would they rise and soar and dive as they
were meant
For their feet were imprisoned in three inches of cement.

The paving where the lawn should be was octagonal
coloured blocks
It had been set out by a craftsman with a little space for rocks
The beauty of the natural stones was spotted as with blight
But on a second glance, I saw that they were painted white.

The rabbits and the gnomes looked on an ornamental pond
More kidney-shaped than oval, geometrics most profound
A perfect arch of stainless steel spanned over to the blocks
And then I saw the plastic stork, where there should have
been hollyhocks.

The orange of the street lamp made the garden kind of glow
And the big green frog was silent, not a petal near its toe
What a way to spend a lifetime, he was thinking to himself
When he could have been much warmer on the garden
centre shelf.

No speck of earth was showing where a daisy could
have grown
No tiny nook or cranny for a seed to find a home
It was spotless, it was perfect, as any eye could see
But no shade would ever gently spread across it from a tree.

A little further down the street behind an old board fence
Stood a cottage that had seen better days, the gate was
even bent
The apple tree had shed its leaves, they lay amongst the grass
The browns and golds all blending, as a hen went clucking past.

A blackbird sang his evening song from an upturned
barrow's leg
The garden line swung in the breeze, dotted here and there with pegs
A hedgehog sniffed along the path and down the cabbage row
If I wished to spend time in a garden
I know where I should go.

Cyril G Payne

122

A GREEN LAND

The land round here is truly beautiful,
the sparsely scattered population kind;
gentle, closely wooded hills
give way to soft green valleys
painted with daisies and dandelions:
In springtime many roads
are framed in yellow
with vibrant daffodils;
May trees clothe themselves
in clouds of clouds of white;
bluebells crowd the woods; rape fields
spread their golden brilliance
in abundance;
bare trees grow their delicate lace
of green, as new leaves open.
Everywhere glorious birdsong
Fills the air.

In summer the emerald deepens
buttercups enhance the roadside colours,
the woods patchworked
with still more varied greens.

Autumn brings its reds and russet browns
until the fallen leaves replace the flowers
with their own short-lived carpet;
each morning the hills are lost in mist –
sometimes it lasts all day.

Last winter the snow
bleached everything white,
then hoar frost struck,
jewelling every branch and blade of grass
with diamond sparkle.

Each season casts is won enchanting spell.
The land round here is truly beautiful.

Jacqui Fogwill

THE PARISH HALL

It was in the year 1907
The year when I was born
The year when I began my life
The village to adorn

I cost $400 to build
A massive sum indeed
But I fulfilled a purpose
It was the people's need

I stand erect and all alone
In the hamlet Pantydwr
For 100 years I welcomed all
To come inside my door

I protected all from raging storms
Of rain, hail, sleet and snow
Also a baking heatwave
Not so very long ago

I am the parish hall
In the hamlet Pantydwr
I feel I've done my duty
For a century and more

Throughout my life I've seen it all
Eisteddfod, teas, elections,
Concerts, dances, bowls,
And other recollections

I served you all through my life
And now must come the end
A new hall now is being built
On that you must depend.

R M Williams

SACRED SHORE

Here in memory a place of poets divine
Of Dylan Thomas, Lewis Carrol, forever mine
I held hands with love, herein joy
In crystal morning skies pastel blue
I walked the lucid mile and a half
By wooden benches row on row
Here I rest with the ghosts of all
In a paradise they did know
Where calm seas in silver spangles met
Crystal mists from the tides below
Cascading the opalescent heights
Conwy Hills lit in shimmering gold
Here in calm dawn's splend'rous light
Such peace I did behold
In beauty, in drifts, mist lured me stay
Where tranquil serenities ebb
On a placid tide in treacle seas
Melting in turquoise web
I dwelled in this purity of light
Holding hands with love I thrived
Within the plaques on benches new
I chose to sit on five
Reading the words from beloved families
The true happiness of family ties
For they have known a haven as I
In the simplicity of gentle tides
Of a constant sea on golden shores
In the mornings of seagulls' cries
Crimson sunsets o'er mountain tops
Where this sacred shore abides
Within the opalescent mists
Rushing hearts to timid tides

Christine Gamble Griffith

THE ROAD TO WALES

The owl hooted eerily in the sky
The field mouse silently gnawed
His banquet consisted of barley and rye
Somewhere a woodpigeon soared

As dawn came over the silent slopes
I tramped my weary way
Something within raised my hopes
And promised a better day

My limbs ached from walking
From Bristol and the west
Ah, you've guessed, my life was tramping
And poaching with the best.

I hailed a passing lorry
And used my hard luck face
The driver said
'Sure mate, sit on this packing case'

As we crossed the River Severn
He spun some lively tales
Of how he'd come from Devon
But had settled now in Wales.

We passed a place called Newport
Then Cardiff came in sight
The castle like a fortress
Silhouetted the morning light

The battlements stood in sharp relief
Against the crimson dawn
The ancient courtyard stretched below
Replaced now by a lawn

I tried to visualise the men
Who once lay down their lives
Who had fought for Henry and Elizabeth
With sabres, swords and knives

From here we went to Margam
Past a big industrial plant
And I began to take an interest
In this land of Dewi Sant.

From there we came to Swansea
Grey in the light of day
But I've learned to love this city
In an adopted sort of way

I love the great big marketplace
Entirely roofed in glass
Where congregating Saturdays
Are every creed and class

The women sitting patiently
Selling cockles in their shells
The interruption frequently
Of St Mary's mid-day bells

But the place which pleases me the most
Is the scenery on the Gower coast
I tell you folks it makes my day
To see the sun go down on Three Cliffs Bay.

So dear friends, if all else fails
Pack up your troubles and come to Wales.

Audrey Morris

LAND OF MY FATHERS

Somewhere in Wales there's a place called Portskewett
When mentioned to strangers nobody knew it
This village of ours may still be a mystery
But believe it or not – it's steeped in history

It still has some of that olde worlde charm
Charles the Second slept at the Manor Farm
Our ancient church stands in all its glory
Next to Harold's castle – another story

Way upon an earthy mound
Stands a Roman burial ground
Excavation found that there
Lay human bones and pottery rare

There's one thing that will never die
The River Severn running by
Ferries once crossed from this port
Now there's transport of a different sort

I look through the back window, I see the Severn Bridge
To the front there's the 'Croeso' right on the ridge
Between the two bridges, Portskewett's right here
Where generations have lived and I hold most dear.

Maureen Pearce-Webb

WINDOWS

In my church there's a beautiful window
Given in memory of someone passed on.
Portraying a life successful and valued –
Leaving behind a pattern of joy.
All through our lives we conquer or struggle
But there's reward when we find success.
Things are not easy, life is demanding
And what's before us we cannot guess.
Down all out streets there are many windows,
Some have dark curtains and shut out the light,
No one can tell what problems are hidden
All we can do is fight for what's right.
When life is dark, we peer through our windows
Nature delights us and makes life worthwhile.
Bad weather hinders, making us nervous,
Then comes the sunshine and we can all smile.
There is reward when we are successful –
Giving our lives the bliss of content.
Knowing we've conquered brings us great pleasure,
Nothing is wasted if life is well spent.

Glenys B Moses

SMILING ON THIS CITY

God smiles today –
I see His face in the clouds . . .
Smiling on this city.
The living and the dead rise
To worship the Master.

>   A sea of glass
>   clear as crystal
>   around the throne

Even Lucifer bows, for he knows
His weapons of mass deception
Will not be sufficient to rule the sanctuary.

>   Seagulls sing like angels
>   the sun floats
>   on a dancing wave

The battle is the Lord's.

Ken Price

MY TOWN

When I was you, I took a look from up above,
I saw a sight I love,
A bay like Naples, that I saw on a postcard years ago,
Why waste money on buses and trains and planes,
Packing cases, changing money,
Waiting in airports with thousands of others, dragging cases
In queues and people with anxious faces, no thanks,
I would rather sit on a mile long promenade, watching the world go by . . .
Didn't cost me anything.
There's a smile on my face and a few bob in my pocket,
I'm on holiday in my town.

Nancy Shields

NEWPORT CITY NEWS

Here we are in Newport
A Welsh city once a town
Though when you tell some people
It raises just a frown

Industrial revolution came
It started such a race
Race was on to produce
Many things at great pace

Newport city of uprising
With chartists and their will
To change the world they live in
Though blood was caused to spill

Collieries" wheels ground to a halt
Clean energy now the fore
Though 'twas tough then being a miner
Before environmental laws

The rivers now run cleaner
Though blackened once by coal
Once thought to be the norm
Before environmental goals.

Stephen Maslen

THE SWAYING OF THE DAFFODILS

The swaying of the daffodils over Wales, vales and hills
There is such beauty around us, a wonder to be seen,
Perfume of the yellow daffodils all around, the air they fill.
Such magnificence the sight and the grass is ever lovely
and green.

The crocuses, their colours, yellow, white, purple and blue.
The splendor of the mountains, the rivers reflect them, they do!
Swaying crocuses and their fragrance, give out their perfume too.
The chirping of the birds and the buzzing of the bees give out tunes anew.

The swaying of the bluebells and primroses dance in spring's warm sun.
Over the mountains in forests, woods and dells they become
They are so lovely and beautiful, they make the heart rejoice.
Then we, His chosen loved ones, listen to His gentle voice.

He planted all the roses, blue, red, yellow and orange too
Their sweet fragrance upon the butterfly for us to enjoy
and we do!
The sparkling of the waterfall as it rushes over mountains,
hills high,
All the wonder of Wales to enjoy, our spirits soar up to the sky.

Wales is so beautiful, it has been put here by God's hands.
All the glory of the flowers and their colours can be seen throughout the land.
The stars up in the heavens and all that twinkles in space
Everything in order, every wonderful thing in God's place.

Our Wales is so wonderful, I'm glad God placed us here.
For when we look upon this beauty we know He's ever near.
We have no reasons to worry or have any doubts or fears
Knowing that our Heavenly Father, He's all in all dear.

Joan McCradie

BRYN EURYN

Bryn Euryn, a hill to the rear of Rhos-on-sea some 350ft high.
From the top a panoramic view of the Conway Mountains,
the river and sea.
A fortification stood at the top, built in the days of Edward I.
Nothing remains today except mounds of grass covering
old walls,
In the same area lies Llys Euryn, a small hill
Where once stood a three-storey building,
Some call it a castle, others a large mansion.
This was the favourite residence of Ednyfed Fychan.
Many families occupied the property but at the end of the Elizabethan age
A phase of life in the area ended and castles were crumbling.
Manor houses and farms took on a new meaning which enlivened the countryside.

Items found during excavation were a brass shoe buckle, gun flints, boars' tusks, part of a
candle snuffer
And a small quantity of coins were found hidden in a wall.

Barbara Heaton

ACERS OF BODNANT

Under a cloudless sky we wandered
in early November;
The sun brought to life
the fallen leaves of the acers.

No other visitors followed this path,
so we had the peaceful beauty
all to ourselves
blood, scarlet, vermilion.

Touched up with orange-yellow,
the carpet glowed.
The copse was lighted
and peace was on Earth.

As we sauntered across the carpet
under the parent trees,
the warmth could be felt,
soothing our feet.

We realised we'd spoken not at all.
This was not a place for words.
We slowly, and sadly, made our way
back to the real world.

Gordon Lowden
Was the author unwittingly composing his own epitaph? For he died soon
afterwards without knowing of its publication.

TREASURES OF TORFAEN

Hard downhill lies a verdant plain
A rolling plain
Its past, its present, will ever remain
Tumbling from uplands comes a rippling rill
Its ancient waters never lie still
A towpath wends to the lock-keeper's cottage
And a white water weir
Where I remember calming a wounded deer

A compass helps one's wonder best
As mountainous Twm Barlwm rises west
And to the east? A feast!
Of greening orchards
See ripening Bramleys and the succulent Cox
But beware! Alongside scurries the Monmouth fox!
Then south to Afon Llwyd the woodland yields
Bending round yellow rape and bursting wheatfields

We listen for the sound of ponies clip-clopping
On our own Rotten Row!
To Meadow Brook – without stopping!
On crisp early morns fully hidden by snow,
Or when autumn's orange sun sets a splendid glow
This fair land welcomes our eyes, ever to range,
With a timeless bond
No force, no power, can ever change.

Ken Marshall

ABER-TAWE (SWANSEA)

Started off little town, Prince of Wales made us a city.
Much has happened, it's now quite pretty.
Good entertainment, few nice shops,
Cafes, restaurants, are the tops.
Liberty Stadium – new hope for sport.
New marina, where the boats are bought.
Child at war-time, things looked bad.
No luxuries, cars or food to be had.
Twenty-first century, we can toy with power.
Top award has been given to our gower,
Out of ashes, our city has risen.
Swansea city has a lot to be given,
On offer, much to be seen,
Beaches, mountains and valleys so green,
Like the gnomes of Zurich, city our dome,
Being Welsh, humble, there is no place like home.

Sheila Donetta

THROUGH THE WOODS WE GO

Through the woods we go,
pass the fields of
wild flowers.
Where the owl makes his home
in the great old oak.
The hares chasing
one another.
Butterflies dancing
in the summer air.
Snails slowly crawling along
leaving behind a silver line.
The caterpillar
munching on a leaf.
Blackbirds nesting
in amongst the tree branches.
Tiny spiders spinning
their silver silk webs.
Bumblebees racing
along as they go about
collecting nectar.
Listening to nature's
song as we go.
Fish below the river's surface.
Weeping willows
creating ripples now and then.
A frog sitting on
his lily pad
waiting for
his next meal.
It's been a lovely walk through the woods
don't you think?

Jessica Stephanie Powell

A RHONDDA VALLEY MORNING

In the morning I climb the hill to watch the rising sun,
speeding up the valley, striking houses, one by one.
Windows in turn, reflect the sun, with a warm and mellow glow,
row after row of golden squares, from grey walls
seem to show.
A bright onrushing tide of light, moving past the
houses of grey,
to reach the fields, and touch the sheep, munching on the hay.
Lighting trees and flowers growing in the dew damp ground,
and spreading a spring fresh feel of newness all around.
The distant sound of a barking dog disturbs the morning air,
clinking bottles play a tune, the milkman's
around somewhere,
Mothers calling sleeping children, breaking their happy dreams,
I smell bacon, eggs, toast and jam, I'm hungry now it seems.
More doors are opening and closing, more folk on the rise,
radios and TVs tuning up, mingling with children's cries.
The school bus engine roars into life, the kids are very slow,
it's eight o'clock, they rush up the h ill, hoping it will not go.
Mothers gossiping, sharing the news, relaxing now at ease,
clothes being hung upon the lines, in the gently
blowing breeze.
The sun is halfway to its peak, the birds are in full cry,
the little village is awake at last under the clear blue sky.

Brian Toomey

WELCOME TO WALES

Our green tumbling hills adorned with graceful daffodils
Breathtaking valleys that run so deep
The view stays in your heart, it is there to keep
Hearty Welsh singers with that thunderous roar
With those wonderful sopranos, elegance galore!
The Welshman's 'caviar' known as laverbread
On a plate served with cockles and bacon not spared
Our Welsh rugby players who are simply the best
They wear the three feathers with pride on their chest
In the Premier League stand our football team
They are the Swans who reign so supreme!
Without very own statue, Dylan Thomas of course
Then there is Ffos Las, where you can be on a horse
Our magnificent castles that stand their ground
Their walls have secrets that leave you spellbound!
Such a choice of beaches, too many to say
With private owned chalets on Caswell Bay
The stunning marina, full of beautiful yachts
Owned by the wealthy who have money pots!
Our fine grand theatre with its lavish décor
Where plays are stage, then so much more
There are tribute bands and hypnotists
Not to mention that wicked witch!
Traditional Welsh ladies in costume and hat
Scrumptious Welsh cakes, reduced in fat
Mouthwatering ice cream from a parlour named 'Joe's'
Come rain or shine it's where everyone goes
A fire-breathing dragon adorns our national flag
While Margam Park has deer, plus a handsome stag
Our very own royal, the Prince Charles of Wales!
Who pulls in the crowds, he never fails
Even the rainfall cannot change my mind
Wales is the finest region you will find.

Andrea Trick

THE BLACK MOUNTAINS OF WALES

Over the mountains, a summer breeze sighs
A whisper of breath under clear blue skies
Deep down in the valley, far reaching below
Sprinkled droplets of gold in the sun's morning glow.

The mountain is still, with the heavens at rest
A time of the day that I so love the best
As I drink in the balm that nature instills
I gaze up in awe at the beautiful hills.

They thrust through the valley and stretch to the sky
On silent wing a lone hawk hovers by
My mind is at peace in the quiet of day
As serenity washes my troubles away.

Wrapped in pockets and folds, little farmhouses stand
Lost to the world on this green fertile land
Sheep steadily munch, playful lambs have been born
Each drenched in the joy of this mystical morn.

But a sour-faced mountain can often be tough
Gripped in jaws of a thunderstorm, cruel and rough
Aggressively wild when blustery winds blow
When the lamp of the storm lights the valley below.

Changes occur as the seasons unfold
From the rich blaze of autumn, to a snap raw and cold
When winter holds court as a powerful king
Then agrees to submit to a soft gentle spring.

There is charm in their magic, nature's contrast we find
A look fresh and vital, a beast savage and wild
They stand as forever, majestic and tall
For strong is the voice of the mountain's call.

Barbara Davies

MY FAVOURITE PLACE

I fell in love with Wales
When I married a Cardiff boy
In spite of my mother's objection
He brought me nothing but joy
You see, I am a Londoner
With family and work going fine
I took my sister for a week in Wales
And met this fellow divine
My mother had a thing about Wales
And nearly had a fit
But I had the loveliest in-laws
And didn't worry a bit
So I lived in this lovely Wales
With mountains and beaches to view
And people so helpful and friendly
With a husband so loving and true
So I didn't miss London at all
With so much in Wales to see
Lovely scenery everywhere
This Wales enchanted me
There's lots of history about this land
With its castles and ancient ways
Its heavenly music and wonderful choirs
I shall stay for the rest of my days.

June Mary Davies

MY PLACE

I'm happy in this place I live,
There's so much beauty here –
Sweet snowdrops in our garden grow,
And a hedge of yellow roses there
In the other garden, and a clematis,
And a lovely silver birch.
In gardens down tree-rich Conway Road,
Blue campanula bells on the wall,
And poppies, orange and yellow.
I've seen a squirrel dart,
When I look through my window
And there is a copper beech, ivy-clad.
Bright-berried holly near us grows,
And down the road in spring,
Daffodils and narcissi;
Later, white and pink-blossomed trees.
(Our shops are good, but fairly 'dear'
A florist changed to a shop for bikes,
Then down the block, some bikes became
A coffee shop for us!)
I am so blessed and I thank God
For this, my place, so very dear.
God is my Saviour, Shepherd, King,
And I know He led me here.

Wendy Prance

JEWELS ON LOAN

Through the darkness of the night
to the deepness of the ocean,
outline of the brooding mountains
landscape awakening to morning light . . .

In the darkness sounds defilter,
in the deepness thoughts abound,
Gazing at the lightening mountains
profound shades of colours silvered . . .

Rambling shore midst sand and pebbles
shapes abound in artistry,
dipping toes in edge of tiding
rain and sun shades creating jewels . . .

Sounds erupting, atmosphere of time
listening to the wind that rumbles,
figures drifting as in days gone by
pirating pots of gold and wine . . .

Watch the sunset in all its glory
skies of Technicolor hues.
Step the bridge that feet have trodden
years of weather have paid its dues . . .

Wildlife singing, trees whispering breeze,
another world, too few see or hear.
Treasured moments, measured time
Should be bottled . . . but 'tis only leased . . .

M L Damsell

TRAETH GWYN, LLANINA

Once we'd take the footpath
through St Ina's churchyard.
Now the path is through the wood,
where the River Llethi runs down to the sea.

In the churchyard the grave
of poet and campaigner Dot Clancy,
dancing shoes and words.
Her funeral overflowing, a trumpeter played
'When The Saints Go Marching In'.

We cross the river
on the wedge of stone and wire,
up steps to the lookout point,
and down to the sea.

Smugglers unloaded booty
took it up through the church into the woods.
From here Dylan Thomas walked into New Quay
composing sentences in his head.

Dogs race around.
Warm sand on our feet,
sea lapping our ankles.

From driftwood, abandoned rope
and beach rubbish we sculpt
a land-locked boat.

'This is my favourite place,' my son says
'The Pirate Beach.'

Sue Moules

PEMBROKESHIRE

(Written in love of my adopted homeland – Pembrokeshire)

Atlantic gust tickles wearily on my ageless face.
I stand upon god's chosen acre.
He touches the waters with golden fingers.
Of all the love of our Maker.

Someone, anyone, tell me I'm wrong.
This beauty fills my eyes with a single tear.
This place must be made from angels.
Crashing of waves which I so revere.

The magnificent unspoilt golden bays.
And the secrets of the hidden coves.
The timeless tales of Celtic legends
And of whispers of hidden treasure troves.

The solitude of the monks upon the Caldey Isle.
To the bustling town of Haverfordwest.
The green fields of patchwork cover
This land I love the best.

Stand out upon Pembroke's ancient castle
And imagine of times gone by.
As a thousand warriors march in siege.
Now only tourists I do spy.

The Tenby beaches both north and south
Fill when sun comes with flaming July.
They stake their claim to every square inch.
Till September waves them goodbye.

Oil rigs fight the waterways
With sailing ships, trawlers and ferry
Where once did great wooden galleons sail
Within them, sailors' rum merry.

Upon the distant horizon embrace
The refineries' towering dark shapes.
Outstretched into the estuary
Their metallic armed jetty drapes

The sun dips over Freshwater West upon the eve.
A little magic fills this sight.
Nature has the last word of the hour
And day slips into night.

So many cast out into the world
To find some other glory.
But most return to this sacred place
To finish up their story.

Stuart Lee Adams

BECKONING ME

In that far-flung place, the hills and vales called me,
Gurgling cascades pouring over my sandaled feet,
Washed leaves on every emerald tree,
In just one day, sunshine, mist, fog, rain, hail, sleet.

Laughing through it all we ran, 'up and down',
Rivers then, sludge, slurping, not swift,
Fern-shimmering fields, new forests, hilltops crown,
Now willful, cheeky, ravenous herons, salmon lift.

Cool, clear flowing through towns, villages, new and old,
They witness the town market of bustle, 'buy and sell',
With bridges, side by side, the senior arched stone, the other, flat, bold,
Deserted coalmines, sentinels with tales to tell.

The struggle to get black gold, the ever-present danger,
Answering the call, I am here in my valley of choirs,
Our jostling, quarrelling terraced houses amaze every stranger,
I recall, neat 'cwtchy' homes with blazing coal fires.

There is a celebrated park, in remembrance of war, lost
loved ones,
The blood sacrifice of fathers, mothers, daughters, sons.
The children grow tall,
Brick by brick building their own memory wall.

Merylrose Sivyer-Dixon

Powys

Warm rain seeps gently
Over soft round hills
Filling a hundred streams
That trickle, tumble, bounce
Down little valleys,
To join the wye
Or mighty river Severn.

Sheep, sheep, more sheep
Drift in white companies
Converting pasture
Into woollen tunics.
The red kites
Soar and glide above,
Seeking the carrion
For their hungry chicks.

The conifers brood grimly
On the peaks
Of ancient mountains
Old as time itself,
Roads twist and wind,
Linking stone villages
Where boys and girls play games
Their mums and dads knew well.

The lilting syllables
Of a different tongue,
The choirs, the music
Of Eisteddfodau,
Define the culture
Of this Celtic world,
A world of mists and mountains
Bards and poetry.

Frank Hooley

GOD'S OWN COUNTRY

God's own country; that has to be the Eden Vale,
Every pasture green, every hill and dale,
Every beck and stream which flow to be
With the River Eden reaching out to the sea.

Protected all around my mountains and hills
With their heather-clad slopes and shimmering rills
Which chuckle as they race to the valley below,
Ensuring that all that is good for us may grow.

If the valley has a queen, it must surely be
The old county town of Westmorland, Appleby,
Where the Eden divides the town in two,
Meandering quietly, but oft' times wrathfully too!

Are those the 'Lambs of God' that we can see;
Winter-coated Herdwick sheep roaming free?
Wild pones too, with thick coats to withstand the cold;
Their rightful home, God's own country, 'twas thus of old.

There are umpteen villages along the valley floor,
And on the fell sides yet even more;
Each with a shop, an inn, church and school;
Each self-sufficient, a hidden gem, a rare jewel.

But times have changed, some village shops have closed;
The little schools too; changes which must have posed
Problems galore for all who live there,
But it's still God's own country, in God's tender care.

Marlene Allen

Heaven On Earth

Beyond the lake auld Skiddaw stands
Here in its rightful place in Lakeland.
It looks so heavenly and so serene;
Nowhere else on Earth can this be seen.

Out on the lake boats are in full sail,
And seeing each other, shout and hail.
If there are any mishaps, they soon get aid
Here in this lovely place that God made.

Near to the lake's shore can be seen
Ducks and swans as they all feed.
Along comes a boat, giving them a fright,
Skipping along the water they take flight.

Surrounded by mountains looking so big
Is the Druids' Circle at Castlerigg.
Looking across at Blencathra I see tracks
Stretching all the way up Saddleback.

Then there's Keswick near Derwent's shore;
Who in this world could ask for more?
A place where visitors can be seen
In this wonderful place fit for a queen.

Further down the valley is Grasmere;
The home of William Wordsworth was here,
The poetry he wrote about this lovely place
Will never ever go out of date.

Passing through Grasmere, Hawkshead lies;
It's to this village I have family ties,
Which keep it deep in my heart and mind
Where my ancestors lived, worked and died.

On reaching Ambleside, have a walk around
And see the lovely shops in the town;
After your visit and you do depart,
Pleasant memories will stay in your heart.

Over Kirkstone Pass down past Brotherswater
Lies the loveliest lake called Ullswater.
Here on its shores William Wordsworth strolled
And wrote about daffodils that looked like gold . . .

At the end of the lake Pooley Bridge stands,
A beautiful village I'm sure God planned.
People from all over the world you'll find
Who leave with memories imprinted on their mind.

When from this life I do depart
With my hand placed on my heart
I'll thank the Lord for this Lakeland;
I am so proud to be an Englishman.

Francis Allen

A LIFETIME OF MEMORIES

I live in South Wales, the land of song
Family and friends, we all belong
To a little town called Barry Docks
With high tides between the gates and locks

Coal was shipped near and afar
Boats would follow the Northern Star
You could cross the docks and touch no water
Step from one boat to another, I told my daughter

The beaches at Barry Island with golden sand
All the visitors thought it was the Promised Land
The fairground going from morning till night
And the haunted house, gave you a terrible fright

Thompson Street was known worldwide
As was Cardiff's Tiger Bay
Friends and neighbours side by side
Some folk left, most wanted to stay

I was a sailor a short time in my life
And never been far from the sea
But I gave it all up, that struggle and strife
Now retired, I'm happy and free.

Anthony Mitchell

WALES

I love this countryside of Wales
With its rolling hills and lovely vales,
Mountains high, rugged and grand,
Rivers that wind through purple moorland.

Castles grim, on high they stand,
Centuries ago guarding the land.
When knight and king quarreled and fought
To rule this land of song and thought.

Across the moors the heather grows
Honeysuckle, foxglove in the hedgerows.
Fields that turn from green to gold,
With corn and wheat, a wealth untold.

Cattle graze on sweet green grass,
Sheep that roam from crag to pass
Mountain ponies, heads held high,
With streaming manes as they pass by.

But most of all I love the woods,
Horsechestnuts with the sticky buds,
Oak, ash and lofty pine,
And the little fir trees that stand in line.

And now that I'm too old to roam
I sit and dream of scenes I've known,
Of lakes and trees, and mountains high,
They're all beloved in my mind's eye.

Joann Littlehales

THE DEMISE OF A BARRY ISLAND SEAGULL

I was driving to work
When I saw it in the gutter
'Only a seagull, a rat with wings'
Is probably what you'll mutter.
But think of what he must have seen
When soaring in the sky,
The swaying trees, the stormy seas,
Sights to make you cry.
Very quick and cheeky
These seagulls tend to be,
They'll take your sandwich from your hand
When you picnic by the sea.
But to see him lying there
In a dirty, bloodied heap,
I think it's really sad,
It makes my poor heart weep.
So have a care for animals and birds
They're part of nature who
Are just trying to survive,
The same as me or you . . .

Ruth Grant

A LITTLE WELSH GIRL – DAISY BELLE

A little girl who looks around
At birds and bees
And all the sounds

Our garden to her is a magic place
And to see the flowers
Brings big smiles to her face

The cows in the fields
The sound of the sea
What a wonderful place
For our little girl to be

It won't be long before she walks
What will she say when she starts to talk?
I think big stories and long-lasting tales
About this wonderful place
We call Wales.

T B Rees

TREASURED MEMORIES

Where are the seasides of long ago?
Ones in memory we used to know
Pleasurable trips when young
Everything there for a day in the sun
Round the fairground would take time
Seeking rides which were good fun
Helter-skelter, the Mouse, scenic railway
And ghost House made us shriek with fright.
Off now for a gentle stroll down the prom
To buy an ice cream, wolf-whistles
Following, footsteps not far behind
Passing the sellers on our way, all
Saleable goods neatly displayed, beach
Accessories, buckets and spades,
Fortune teller plying her trade, various
Seafood cockles, mussels, prawns set
In disposable trays
Sticks of rock, lollipops, popcorn also
Candyfloss, that end stall sold the lot.

Down below the sands looked busy
A crowd had gathered to watch Punch and Judy.
The donkeys were carrying rides back and forth
With children crying to have a go.
Sandcastle fortresses being built
Kept others amused, while
Dads worked hard shoveling sand for their use.

Far out to sea a steamship in passing was
Belching smoke from its funnels, that seemed
To darken the horizon
Suddenly a heavy shower started
Sending everyone running searching for shelter.
Typical summer holiday weather.

These treasured memories known
The beaches played upon and loved at home
Familiar sights now no more
Never once gave thought to leave
To desert this land for distant dreams.

Valerie Thompson

A GREENOCK WELCOME

Welcome tae Greenock
On the bonnie banks o' Clyde
Where ye'll find yersel' surrounded
By nature's splendours far and wide

There are lots o' lovely sights tae see
Places of interest tae
Ye can go explore
Tae yer heart's content
Frae Port Glesga tae Cardwell Bay

Ye'll find the Oak Wall wi' shops galore
The art gallery and museum as well
The Cross O' Lorraine at the top o' Lyle Hill
A reminder o' war tae tell

Ye can walk along the esplanade
Doon past the Greenock Boat Club
Then stroll aroon the Battery Park
And see lots o' folk wi' their dugs

And remember tae bring yer swimmin' gear
For a dunk in the Gourock pool
Or go fur a trip wi' Cally Mac
On a steamer tae bonnie Dunoon

Hope ye've enjoyed
Braw Inverclyde
That ye've many a tale tae tell
Haste ye back, we'll see ye again
God speed and keep ye well

Elizabeth Watters

TIPTON OF PAST

Being born in 'Tippun', gives rise to the thought, *being thick in arm, thick in head!*
They think with their brawn and not with their brain!
Of course, this isn't strictly true – it only affects the few!
Their speech can be 'Yo dow, yo dae, yo bin, yo bay' but this dates back to 'olde English', you know!
To the point, direct to speech, all these characters, who are supposed to be thick in arm, thick in head
Of course, this is fading, with the rise of education and 'modern-ness' – 21st century living.

Of old, picking coal, to keep the children warm, as well for cooking, to keep 'em fed
Times were hard, many men breathed the dust and sweat their blood and all for a paltry bob or two
'Wash days', shared in the brew house, their weekly wash, they took turns to do – no washing machines then – just brute force!
Cold water from the tap, if lucky, they would have a bit of coal backed up with 'slack' to burn, to get the water hot
Summer was fine to dry their washing but when winter came, not everyone would be clean, 'lack of 'was the order
of the day

Some lived well – 'the well-to-do', the bosses, some moderate but most had hardly anything at all
Families, twelve, thirteen, fifteen – how did they feed them all? And all because the candles had to be put out, for they had to last the week!
No one was proud to pick up and finish an apple core
No one was proud to ask for the bruised left upon the stall
No one was proud to wait to the very last, to see what was left and what the shopkeeper would let them have
Everything was eaten, everything they could get, from ears, feet, head and guts! Long lasting were the stews!

Nothing strange about three in a bed or top to toe on a
straw mattress
Some poor souls had to sleep on the floor, their one and only coat – their blanket
Nothing in their belly to go to school, relying on the kindness of a few, who would give a piece of bread
Shoes on feet, too big, too small, taped or in holes
A coat bought when small, had to be worn till tall, sleeves halfway up their arms – just imagine the humiliation
Trousers, with patched up holes, again, worn till looking
like shorts
Being fat, didn't hardly exist, because being poor kept
them thin.

Poverty kept them sharp, not too proud to scour a dustbin
Every week, the 'pawn shop' would call, popping in their father's one and only suit or

whatever, to bring in a coin or two, to last them through – then borrow another to get them out – never out of debt

A blown up pig's bladder, blown up till tight – this gave the lads a bit of pleasure to kick

A 'button on a string' tap, tap on a window but there was no one about! Only the victim's shout, 'I'll tan yer hide if I catch yer – yer little buggers!'

Pleasures were simple made up games, running about, always out, in the smoggy industrial air, swimming in the dirty 'cut'

Yes, 'poverty' on our Tipton streets and not so long ago

But men were men, a spade a spade and the women, only good at the daily scrubbin', beating the rug made out of material scraps – no high flyin' careers then! Just daily scrattin' to keep alive

But now, those men and women are no longer here but the stories of their lives will live on, through 'Tippun' hearts, for that is how life was

New people coming from everywhere, who have no knowledge of the poverty years – coal bonks, foundry sweat, dirt, grime, obnoxious air, canal lives, cholera, typhus, no running water, infantile early deaths – aren't they lucky?

Barbara Fletcher

ROUNDING THE BAY AT NEWGALE

Anticipated joy, surprise
Every time
At the bend at Newgale.
A fleeting glimpse of water
Between the headlands.
Then wide sea, islands,
Then the whole panorama of the bay.

Delight in every kind of weather
Sunlight on water,
Mist on the headlands
Or glowering storm clouds gathering

Eclipsed the thoughts of yesterday
Or what is yet to come.
Beauty, balm to the soul,
The joy is now.

Fran Barker

THE WAIF OF KINMEL BAY

The sea is a bed of slate today
Running with corrugated cream.
Swirling around the lips of the bay
A wrack stitched meandering seam.
Grey old men in haunched overcoats
Rumble in tumbrils above
The limp-sailed orphaned fishing boats
Abandoned by the wind to face
A flatline, dead horizon braced
With the beaten rays of a solstice sun.
A woven mesh in crimson spun.

Here is the bay where they came to play
Camped on the wind-besom'd, butterscotch sands
Like a Bedouin tribe on holiday
Who followed their hearts to this Promised Land.
To conjure a trick with a single spade
Building pyramid castles with serpentine moats.
To clamber the sculpturesque barnacle reefs
Surveying their kingdom like obdurate goats.
To stalk the dunes through their emerald sway
Where rabbit and snake rummage and rake.
And the ravens and rooks in the shadowlight pray
Their requiem rites for the death of each day.

I walk through the voices in the echoing void
Of these who were here the summer before.
My senses invisibly toyed
By a mirage of memories; a phantom encore.
Here have I learnt the colour of sound
I have listened to pebble and shell.
All these ancients I have found
Holding time in their eternal spell.
A time when no man walked these shores
To devour the fruit and the feather.
Leaving not a spoor to be traced
Nor his toxic shadow tethered.

Still, who would deny them their pleasure? Not I just leave me a day such as this
To walk the strand and its treasure.
That which I know yet they rarely measure.
Measure the turn of the clocking tides
At Mother Moon's behest.
Each season's kaleidoscope skies.
The mantles of mist from the lungs of the sea

By the sun, in its gilded monstrance, blest
Like the sails of a clipper that silently plies
Its cargo of shrouds dressing me.
So, I may stray, the waif of the bay
With the chains of my spirit cut free.

Philip J Mee

CLWYD: GOLDEN LAND

Clwyd, most northerly of the Cymru fold,
A bastion wall to hold back the sea,
Her fields resplendent with Welsh gold,
This is what Clwyd means to me.

The Silurian epoch named after our tribe,
Who became the Clwydii, the spearmen bold,
Succumbing not to Roman and Viking bribe,
Only by blood would our birthright be sold.

Mountain and valley, river and vale,
Mining for bronze, for slate and for lead,
Farming, both arable and animal still prevail,
Good golden gran giving, both ale and bread.

Clear crystal lakes where monsters still hide,
Rivers teaming with game, fish and eels,
Ragged mountains where dragons reside,
Fishermen struggle home with bursting creels.

Long empty beaches where no foot has yet trod,
Red kites and eagles wheel overhead in the sky,
Sheep gently grazing on salty green sod,
While clouds like ships' sails go scudding by.

Villages and towns where the welcome is kept,
Taverns and hotels to tend to your needs,
Rain washed the streets and the lanes while you slept,
The tide now spent, noisily recedes.

Come here to Clwyd for stays short and long,
We will keep a welcome in the hills and our hearts,
Come see our land of the bard and of song,
Once seen you will love it and never depart.

Bill Hayles

THE MAEHOR

The Maehor low in the water
a black silhouette, against a yellow sky
a vague shadow looming out of the haar
a chameleon, changing with light and weather
almost in touching distance of the shore.
The tower light flashes where the fishing grounds used to be.

Where shipwrecks, sailors, airmen, spirits of the dead let be,
almost forgotten heroes, lie in fifty fathoms of water
near to the Lothian coast, but nearer to the Fife shore.
A gentle breeze wafts the pungency of cliff birds up
into the sky,
minutes later the island changes quickly with the weather,
enveloped now in dense water from the east coast haar!

North and south foghorns boom out their haunting sound in the haar
A warning to ships, where they ought not to be.
No sooner does the mist arrive, then another change
in the weather.
Towering high in the River Forth, it still lies low in the water,
it gleams snowy-white like an iceberg in winter, against a stormy sky
only five miles to Skin Fast Haven, the nearest to any
coast shore.

The Maehor seems to alter shape from each town on the East Neuk shore
Other times invisible, due to the east coast haar
then reappears to break the North Sea horizon where the sea meets the sky.
It's east of here, many years ago, the fishing used to be.
Now they travel further afield to the grounds of deeper water
where they dance with death in the great North Sea, in all kinds of weather.

There for several thousands of years, in all seasons and weather
many invasions by Vikings and Picts landed on its shore.
A one-sided victory over peace-loving monks, where corpses lay on land and water.
On bright sunny days we forget the past, to be reminded on the days of grey haar.
Battles were fought with England here, but hardy seamen, the Scots proved to be.
Mysteries, myths, truth and history go hand in hand with a real and ethereal sky.

The Battle of the May, remembered by some, mayhem under a winter's sky
Boats, subs destroyed, over a hundred crew lost in normal weather!
No enemy ship took part, the Admiralty kept quiet and 'let it be'
With a head-on collision in pitch-dark, no one survived to reach any shore.
Wrapped in secrecy, completely hidden, like the May itself in a grim grey haar!
This catastrophic event, the lives that were lost in the North Sea's dark water.

The Maehor, a black silhouette against a yellow sky, almost in touching distance of the shore
A chameleon changing with light and weather, sometimes invisible due to the east coast haar!
The tower light flashes out to where fishing grounds used to be, and where many lives were lost in the deep North water . . .

James Fraser

SUMMERS' SUMMONS

Gliding smoothly on speedy wheels,
Unimpeded by congested roads,
'Redskin' skims between the hills,
Bound for Glasgow with the post.

A magic journey with entrancing scenes
Beckons the wee van further along,
Pulled by a tarmac thread that gleams
After a summer's rain, not long gone.

Bushes and bracken adorning verges
And leafy limbs of bordering trees
Envelop travelers with onward urges,
Waving buoyantly in the passing breeze.

Weaving its sinuous turning way,
In gentle bends the course flows on.
Redskin makes it seem like play.
Hugging the curves and holding strong.

Leaving village crossroads far behind,
Nature awaits us with even more delights.
Here in a glen browse many doe and hind
And velvet antlered stags engage in fights.

The road narrows and slips into shadow,
Beneath the cover of a forest canopy
And skirts alongside glistening waters below,
That leafy foliage won't quite let us see.

Left at the Tarbet corner with no delay,
Sparkly loch views drift from sight.
Quickening the pace on the straight away,
Swiftly moving, red bird takes flight.

Grand old wall zips by as it rambles along,
Heading towards the golf club's entry gate.
No time at all to stroll across a grassy lawn
Driver and driven must never be late.

Spilling out into the motorways' flow
Like a school of metallic fish,
Each who've waited for the moment to go,
Circle the roundabout with a swish.

The rhythm of four wheels turning round
Careful to watch the speed and obey
Matches every other car, all city bound
Advancing down the dual carriageway.

Running with the pack, going like the wind,
Passing through Milton and across the bridge,
Now onto the M8, curling each bend,
Exit 15 – Springburn just over the ridge,

Redskin arrives at her destination.
Journey's end is close at hand.
Mail bags received with much elation,
On time and that's just grand!

Isolde Nettles MacKay

My Favourite Spot

There's water as far as the eye can see
This is a favourite spot for me
The Atlantic Ocean round the Irish shore
On a private beach . . . who could ask for more?
Just to wander barefoot on the sand
To witness all around . . . God's hand.
I lose all stress amid this peace
The worries of my life just cease.
Early morning is the best time of day
Before any people come this way,
The rocks, the mountains, ocean and sand
Are all so wonderful and grand.
This is the scene I call to mind
When I want to leave my troubles behind
I close my eyes and I can recall
This lovely spot in County Donegal.

Mary Anne Scott

MEMORIES FROM 88-YEAR-OLD BESSIE

It was just an old-fashioned farmhouse known as 'Ironbrae'
When I was only five-years-old I did go there to stay
With sister Mary, brothers Bill and Bob, Mum and Dad there too
They will live with me forever in my memory that is true

With six pigs in the piggery and chickens in the pen
Wire fence all round them and we never lost a hen
With fresh eggs to go with bacon on Sunday morning
what a treat
Porridge always on weekdays all good enough to eat

When you reach the age of 88 all these things come to mind
I wonder if there's more like me with thoughts of a
certain kind

No toilet where you pull a chain, nothing fancy I can tell
As someone when the bucket was full had to empty the pail

Cut up newspapers on the walls that you could sit and read
All of yesterday's news and adds – some were happy and some were very sad

You cannot sit out there for long cos someone would
come and call
Come in and wash the pots and pans and no papers on the wall

We also had a great big pool, we all called it 'the dam'
The ducks all swam around it and we said it was glam
It was so very useful because we had a mill
When the sluice from the dam was open it ground the corn with a will

The days at school were wonderful I loved it every day
We had a wonderful dominie, his name was Mr Dey
We had to walk three miles to school, it really was a pleasure
Along with all our pals that we had made walking was something to treasure
I never ever was late for school or ever days at work
Because when I became nurse, no duties I would shirk

When work was done and time for bed by this time our family was six
We stood behind each other, folks thought it was a fix

One by one we kissed Mum and Dad and all said goodnight to each other
A potty was ready for one and all as outside was too
much bother

I canna hae a bath the nicht there's nae enough hot water
Well we just have to hae a right good dicht though it be
son or daughter

I hope you like this poem for you
It has given me such pleasure
I'm 88, that's a lot of memories
That I will always treasure.

Elizabeth Hassall

FORWARD POETRY INFORMATION

We hope you have enjoyed reading this book - and that you will continue to enjoy it in the coming years.

If you like reading and writing poetry drop us a line, or give us a call, and we'll send you a free information pack.

Alternatively if you would like to order further copies of this book or any of our other titles, then please give us a call or log onto our website at www.forwardpoetry.co.uk

Forward Poetry Information
Remus House
Coltsfoot Drive
Peterborough
PE2 9BF
(01733) 890099